Principles of Applied Stupidity

Principles
of
Applied
Stupidity

How to Get and Do More
by
Thinking and Knowing Less

Justin Locke

version 4.0

Printed in the USA

ISBN: 978-0-615-20792-6

Published by

Justin Locke Productions
Waltham, Massachusetts

www.justinlocke.com

Also by Justin Locke:

Real Men Don't Rehearse
*(Adventures in the Secret World
of Professional Orchestras)*

Family concert works:

Peter VS. the Wolf

The Phantom of the Orchestra

To order a copy of *Real Men Don't Rehearse*, or to read the
scripts of the family concerts and see information about
renting these programs for live performance, visit the Justin
Locke Productions website at **www.justinlocke.com**

Introduction

We live in a society where all things smart and intelligent are good, and anything that is dumb or stupid is bad.

But wait a minute. You probably know many highly intelligent people who are struggling just to get by. Worse, you probably know several C students who have risen quickly and easily to the heights of wealth and power . . . and all too often, they are your boss or your biggest client. What is wrong with this picture?

Strange though it may seem, intelligence is not all that it is cracked up to be. At the same time, stupidity, while much maligned, is often a highly effective method of achieving success.

On the following pages, you will be invited to re-examine your concepts of "intelligence" and "stupidity." You will discover how "intelligence" can be extremely limiting. You will also discover how you can use supposedly "stupid" behaviors to achieve remarkably positive results. (You will also learn how to recognize these highly effective "stupid" techniques, so that others cannot get away with using them on *you*.)

The concepts in this book are really quite simple. In fact, most of them are about simply re-acquiring skills you already possessed when you were two years old. The most difficult part is facing the fearful sense of shame and disapproval that we have been taught to associate with the word "stupid."

The word "stupid" has many meanings. We tend to use the

word "stupid" to define anything that is outside of the "norms" of conventional wisdom. This often includes any different perspective, idea, or thought process that might lead you to an answer that differs from the answer in the teacher's guide. This word gets used a lot, partly because the power of this word's implicit contempt is often stronger than any logical argument.

Well, things are about to change. Once you take a good long look at the total illogic of how we use the word "stupid," you will become impervious to the insidious fear-mongering power of this word. This will give you much greater freedom of thought and action. You will also re-discover something else that you inherently understood when you were two years old: instead of being a source of shame or embarrassment, all the many things you don't know or understand are a source of unlimited power and possibility.

In addition, we humbly submit to you, dear reader, that some of the parts of yourself that you have been told are "stupid" are actually some of the best, the most valuable, and the most interesting parts of yourself. Hopefully, this book will remove some of the fear that may be keeping you from taking full advantage of them.

The word "stupidity" is based on the Latin word "stupidus," meaning "to be astonished." Once you get past all the negatives you have been taught about this word, you may very well be astonished at what *The Principles of Applied Stupidity* can do for you.

--JL

Part One:

Early Research in the Science of Stupidity

"The show was fresh because neither one of us knew how a half hour was done."
                    –Larry David, Co-Creator of "Seinfeld"

Once upon a time there was a young man who was somewhat lost and just generally down on his luck. He was a recent college dropout, working odd jobs, when one day a friend took him along on a trip to a local public access television station. As he made idle chitchat with the receptionist, he was informed, much to his amazement, that if he wanted to, he could come in and play with all the cameras and editing equipment. They would even teach him how to use it. For free.

This young man had often dreamed of working in some glamourous profession like television. Of course, any glamourous profession is generally highly competitive and almost impossible to break into; but here was an opportunity to actually do it. There was no money, but hey, it was television.

For the next year or so, instead of taking classes, he took the "learn by doing" approach. He read no books, he just figured things out by turning the knobs. He fumbled around with making extremely silly projects, all of which were highly amateurish. Then one day another friend of his, who worked for a fund-raising company, said to him, "You make videos, right?" He wasn't really paying attention, so he just answered, "Yeah." And the friend said, "Well, my company needs a video to raise money for a hospital on Nantucket. Why don't you make it for us?" Without thinking too much about it, he said, "Sure."

Before we go on, it might be worth mentioning that, if this young man had gone about being a video producer the "correct way," he no doubt would have paid a lot of his own money to go to

11

some sort of video production school. And no doubt, since all schools are based on the premise that the teachers know more than the students, the first thing he would have learned at such a school would have been how smart his instructors were, and how dumb he was in comparison. He would have quickly learned just how totally unskilled, unschooled, and unqualified he was for any actual professional video production work. And of course, if he had known just how unqualified he was, his conscience would have forced him to turn down this job offer.

However, this is something of a moot point, because if he had been enrolled in such a school, he would have been completely surrounded by other wannabe video producers; therefore he never would have met someone in another line of work who needed his services in the first place.

So as it turned out, his lack of knowledge and schooling actually helped him to get his first real "break," i.e., an actual paying client, which, by the way, is the hardest part of the video business. Or any other business for that matter.

At some point he was told that John Chancellor (who was then the co-anchor of NBC Nightly News) was going to narrate the show, as he was a Nantucket summer resident. Our freshly minted young producer just assumed that Mr. Chancellor was going to send over an audio tape of himself reading the narration. No big deal.

As things got nearer to the shoot day . . . oops. It was suddenly made clear that no, John Chancellor was *not* going to send a tape of the narration. Instead, he was going to make a special trip, and show up on Nantucket on the shoot day to appear on camera.

Let's take a look at this situation. Here it was, this fellow's very first time producing and directing a professional video, and right out of the box he found himself working with the co-anchor of NBC Nightly News. Today, this would be like working with Tom Brokaw.

Now again, if he had possessed any knowledge or experience at all, he would have been very nervous, as he would have known that he was totally unqualified to do the job. But he had no knowledge or experience, and therefore had no idea of how unqualified he was, so he wasn't nervous at all. He figured, he watched five hours of TV every day, so how hard could it be? He had no consciousness of there being any reason not to do it, so yippee, off everyone went to Nantucket.

Now you might think that he was courting disaster, and perhaps he was, but a series of remarkable events transpired:

In the first three minutes of the shoot day, it quickly dawned on the video crew that they had yet another clueless director/producer on their hands (a common experience amongst true professionals). Realizing that this guy was totally useless, the crew became completely empowered. They took over and ran the whole operation. Also, since they found this guy's incompetence to be so objectionable, they wanted to get the day over with as soon as possible. This resulted in the crew moving with lightning speed, taking total initiative throughout the day, never slowing down to ask questions that they already knew the answers to. Even better, the crew's collective disgust for his lack of training was a bonding force that overcame any of their interpersonal differences, so they all worked together magnificently.

(Some people study team management techniques for years, trying to learn how to do what this guy did in less than 10 seconds, on his first time out.)

And as far as Mr. Chancellor was concerned, whenever he had

a question like "Where would you like me to stand?" our first-time director/producer would reply, "Oh, I don't know . . . where would you *like* to stand, Mr. Chancellor?" Since he had no opinions of his own and agreed with everything that everyone said 100% of the time, John Chancellor came away thinking this guy was remarkably humble for someone so talented, brilliant, professional, and great to work with.

And by the way, a little epilogue: when you want to raise money for the only hospital on Nantucket, well, since some of the richest people on the planet spend their summers there, you can generally raise as much money as you want in about 20 minutes. This young fellow had no clue of what he was doing, but the whole thing was a rousing success. He went on to a whole new career in video production.

The crew still rolled their eyes when he called them for another video project, but greed being what it is, they always took the job and showed up, even though they knew they had to work twice as hard.

What did he do to achieve this grand success? Did he study hard and try to impress everyone? No. Quite to the contrary, he got the gig largely by just hanging out in the bar in his health club. And once he had the job, he made it quite clear that he had no idea what he was doing. This gave everyone permission to help him. By looking so pathetic, he actually compelled everyone to contribute their best efforts, as they all had to compensate for his gross incompetence. In other words, he succeeded by using total stupidity.

* * *

Here is another story of stupidity in action:

This story concerns a high school student who had very poor grades. He wasn't "stupid" per se; he just didn't have any interest in most of the subjects. Anyway, when it came time to apply to college, at first he didn't bother. Finally, months after everyone else had applied to college and received their scholarships, he was persuaded by a guidance counselor to submit an application to the local state university. He sent it in a week late, with little enthusiasm. He assumed, given his gruesome grades and woeful attendance record, that he had no chance of being accepted to college. Also, he had no money for tuition, so the whole exercise seemed doubly pointless, but he went through the motions and applied for a scholarship anyway.

Well guess what. That year, the college's admission committee had been so picky that they had fallen short on filling all the available slots. Large universities have quotas to fill, and they suddenly found themselves desperate to fill the empty spaces at the last minute, so . . . When this guy's application came in, even though it was a week late and he had gruesome grades, the university accepted him immediately. That was not the end of it. It turned out that the scholarship committee had been very parsimonious (that means cheap) that year in handing out money to all the eager beaver on-time applicants, so they had a bunch of dough left over. As you know, if a bureaucrat doesn't spend all of his or her total annual allotment, they get less money next year, so they handed this guy a full scholarship. Tuition, room, board, everything.

We tend to think of such phenomena as being the result of dumb luck, but they're not. It's the power of stupidity at work.

*   *   *

Here is a story of how stupidity allowed one doctor to get into his preferred specialty:

This fellow was already a doctor in another area, but he wanted a change. One day he heard that a slot had opened up in a training program for the specialty he wanted to enter. This was a much sought-after specialty, so there was lots of competition; however, he was completely unaware of this fact. Worse, he failed to read the fine print in the announcement about all the requirements for filling out forms, etc. etc. So, on the day of the application deadline, he just sauntered into the office of the person in charge, and casually announced that he was there to enter the training program in the specialty. Again, he had no idea that hundreds of other people (who were far more qualified and experienced than himself) had also applied for the position.

His lack of awareness of the difficulty in getting this position was misinterpreted as confidence. Also, the person who was in charge of picking someone for the one open slot was an avid golfer. He was not thrilled about having to give up an entire summer weekend of golf in order to slog through the massive pile of 200 applications sitting on his desk. So he just gave this guy the position on the spot, tossed all the paper applications, and headed to the links.

If this doctor had done the things correctly, he never would have had the opportunity to enter the specialty of his choice so easily.

This is just one more example of how the Principles of Applied Stupidity can work magnificently, when intelligence and diligence are useless or even counter-productive.

*　　*　　*

Here is yet another story of stupidity in action:

There was a teenager whose high school was not only boring, it was also unsafe. It was a little like being in prison from eight to four each day. He just couldn't take it any more, so at the start of his sophomore year, he simply stayed in bed each morning as the bus came and went. It was not a willful conscious act, but after two months of this daily bus-missing ritual, the end result was that he had dropped out of school.

His parents eventually figured out what was going on. They couldn't bear the embarrassment of having a son who was a high school dropout, so a deal was struck where he would go back to school . . . but now he would attend a hoity-toity *private* high school.

Talk about your changes of scenery. There were teachers who actually cared if he lived or died. There were gorgeous girls . . . who had all of their teeth. No study halls, no knives, and no bullies taking one's lunch money. It was great. It was so much fun that he went on to graduate *cum laude*.

There is no way he would have had that private school opportunity if he had not dropped out of public school first. By not doing things "correctly," this resulted in immensely superior resources being immediately handed to him. This is just one more example of what can happen when you access the power of stupidity.

*   *   *

To be honest, the stories you have just read were not examples of Applied Stupidity. They were stories of *genuine* stupidity.

It certainly would be great if you could rely upon your own innate stupidity to achieve similar successes. Unfortunately, it is pretty much impossible to maintain one's inherent natural stupidity in a society that is obsessed with educating you right from the get-go. You are probably already too intelligent and informed to ever hope to replicate this technique for instant success. However, by learning the essential properties of stupidity, you will find that it is quite possible to *emulate* being in a state of natural stupidity, and this will allow you to achieve similar results. This is why we call it *Applied* Stupidity.

This is not so much about *learning* about stupidity as it is about *un*learning your intelligence. In fact, everything in this book is about doing less, knowing less, and most of all, about *thinking* less.

By itself, this is all incredibly easy and simple. However, undoing all the damage done to you by years of education will require some initial remedial effort. To start you off, on the following pages you will be introduced to the Basic Principles of Applied Stupidity. These basic principles may run slightly counter to some of the common presumptions you may have regarding the virtues of intelligence, as they examine the true meanings of the words "smart" and "stupid." (If it gets dry or dull, please feel free to skip them and come back later.) After this section, the real fun starts, as the Advanced Principles will show you the many ways in which stupidity can be used to great effect in real-life situations.

Note, for your convenience and reference, all of the Principles are listed at the end of book.

Part Two:

Basic Principles of Applied Stupidity

"For me, it's been a help not knowing too much, so I can rely on my instincts."

> *—Simon Cowell, one of the most famous and successful pop music producers in the world, after admitting that he can't play an instrument, sing, or read music.*

Principle #1:
The *Absence* of Thought and Information Is Just as Powerful as the *Presence* of Thought and Information

You may recall doing this classic high school science class experiment:

Your goal is to place a hard-boiled egg inside a milk bottle. To do the experiment, you take a glass milk bottle, and you put some paper inside of it. You then drop a lit match into the bottle. When the paper starts to burn, you place the (peeled) hard-boiled egg on the top of the bottle.

At first, nothing much will happen. But when the fire goes out, the hot air inside the bottle will begin to cool and contract. This will result in there being less air pressure inside the bottle. Next, with a very satisfying "foop" noise, the greater pressure of the outside air will force the egg into the bottle.

If your goal was simply to stuff the hard-boiled egg into the bottle, okay, you wouldn't need the fire; you could just chop up the egg and stuff it into the bottle in bits and pieces . . . but that's the hard way. Here, the lessening of the air pressure in the bottle accomplishes the task easily and immediately. The presence of "nothingness" puts massive forces—in this case, the earth's gravitational pull upon the atmosphere—at your beck and call.

This, in an eggshell, is a prime illustration of the power of non-thought and non-information. The absence of thought or knowledge functions very much like a vacuum. Rather than being an inert or passive state of affairs, the absence of thought and/or information immediately draws all sorts of energy and material to itself.

For all of the constant emphasis on filling your mind with thought and information, if you do the opposite, and create an absence of thought and information, that mental emptiness is itself a powerful force, and cannot be ignored. When that vacuum is created, all sorts of new information and resources will immediately be drawn to you. Just as the earth's gravitational pull on the atmosphere pushed that egg into the bottle for you, when your mind creates a vacuum of thought and information, forces just as great will come into play. People around you will instantly sense that mental vacuum, and will inexorably be forced to respond to it. This is just the beginning of what the power of Applied Stupidity can do for you.

Principle #2:
Everyone Is a Genius.

You have probably been taught all of your life to think of your mental abilities in comparative and competitive terms, so you may find this principle to be a bit shocking. It may sound to you like some sort of attack on your hard-won status, or perhaps a kind of intellectual socialism. Actually, it's quite the opposite. We beg your brief indulgence as we explain:

One of the greatest handicaps placed upon us by "smartist" culture is the idea that intelligence can be codified into one single standard. We have "standardized IQ tests" designed to figure it out, and supposedly, everyone in the world can be equally and fairly measured and ranked by this standard.

This system *would* make sense if we were all pretty much the same. However, like it or not, human minds vary widely in their unique abilities and proclivities. Trying to measure all of our intellects on one scale is like putting a weightlifter and a figure skater in the same competition. It's all apples and oranges and kumquats, but even so, an awful lot of people subscribe to the notion that such universal rankings can be made.

(Even if you don't buy into this system, you are surrounded by people who do, so it's not something you can easily ignore. Also, as you may have noticed, those who subscribe to this notion are extremely sensitive about where they are in the pecking order.)

Since we are all exposed to this system before we are old enough to be able to question it, it is possible that you, dear reader, may have some unresolved personal issues in the realm of how your "intelligence" was once unfavorably rated on this theoretical scale by some faculty factotum of a government-run institution of learning. So just to set the record straight, no matter what your test scores may have been, you are not stupid. In fact, if you are reading this page, you are a genius. Monkeys are pretty smart, and none of them can do what you're doing right now, which is reading a book.

No one thinks about this very much, but in the first five years of your life, along with learning how to walk, you also mastered all the complex physical skills involved in talking—i.e., coordinating your lungs, vocal cords, jaw, teeth, tongue and lips–in order to form words. This says nothing about all the brainwork involved in language acquisition; from a dead start, you learned 80% of your language skills before you ever went to school.

Anyone who has learned to talk has exceeded the technical skill of the greatest violin virtuoso in the world. This means you.

When you start to shift your focus away from anxiety over how you rank against all your supposed intellectual competition, and you accept the fact that no one is stupid and everyone is a unique genius, guess what? You have eliminated any possibility that you can ever be stupid, and better yet, you have also automatically and effortlessly accepted yourself as a genius.

Principle #3:
"Stupid" Does Not Mean Stupid.

Hopefully you have never experienced anyone telling you that you are "stupid," but if you have, you are in pretty good company. Thomas Edison and Albert Einstein were both considered to be stupid when they were children. And what do you suppose some folks thought of Bill Gates when he dropped out of college to start selling a product no one had ever heard of?

The word "stupid" is officially defined as somehow having inferior cognitive/mental abilities, but this is not its primary meaning. In its most common use, the word "stupid" is simply an expression of disapproval. You could be absolutely brilliant, with an IQ of 300, but if you do something that someone else finds to be confusing, frightening, or annoying, you risk being told you are "stupid."

The real emotional impact of this word comes from its implication that our actions are socially unacceptable. Disapproval and rejection are, of course, very painful experiences, and that pain often blinds us to what is really going on.

When someone disapproves of what you are doing, even though they may express this feeling by saying you are "stupid," this has absolutely nothing to do with your innate intellectual capabilities. Recognizing that this word is almost always used as an expression of fear or confusion (or as an attempt to belittle or intimidate you) and is not any kind of objective measurement of your mental abilities, is key to utilizing the power of Applied Stupidity.

Principle #4:
"Smart" Does Not Mean Smart.

You may assume that when someone says you are "smart," they are recognizing and complimenting your superior mental capabilities. This may be the case some of the time, but most of the time, this word means something else altogether. When someone says you are smart, usually what they are really saying is, "I approve of what you are doing, as it agrees with my values and world view."

In other words, to be "smart" means having awareness of, and being obedient to, outside standards. Therefore, to be "smart" really means being an eager conformist.

It is important to note that "smart" is only seen as a good thing by others when it stays within very strict limits. While everyone knows it's a bad thing if you are not smart enough, it is also a bad thing if you are *too* smart. In the latter case, being called smart is no longer a compliment. Instead, you are called a wise guy, a smart aleck, a know-it-all, a geek, or an evil genius. Brilliant perhaps, but not smart. Anything that displeases people, no matter how righteous or brilliant, is not smart.

Approval from others is important, so of course we all like to be told that we are smart. However, your social acceptance is rarely, if ever, based on an objective rational assessment of your mental capabilities. Instead, when someone says you are smart, you are being told that you have met (and not exceeded) the community's standards for what they feel comfortable with. In other words, your "smartness" is a measurement of how agreeable your behavior is to the person doing the measuring.

Principle #5:
The Fear of Looking Stupid
Is an Enormous Force.

You probably remember the Hans Christian Andersen fairy tale *The Emperor's New Clothes*. In the story, two swindlers come to town and let it be known that they can make beautiful clothes, so fine and so beautiful that "stupid people" cannot see them. Of course, there are no clothes to be seen, but the fear of "looking stupid" is so great and so ubiquitous that no one dares to challenge them. Instead, everyone just goes along and pretends that they can in fact see the invisible clothes. And as you probably recall, the story ends with the most powerful man in the empire parading down Main Street in his underwear—in other words, *really* looking stupid.

Because the invocation of the word "stupid" is really a statement that another human being deems you to be socially unacceptable, it is a terrible thing to hear. It brings up many powerful associations of shame and embarrassment, even for those who scored 1600 on the SAT. Certainly, we all want to avoid looking stupid, or heaven forbid, doing anything stupid, as this invites blanket disapproval of our peer group.

However, as the fairy tale teaches us, this terror of looking stupid can get out of hand. For one thing, there is no objective standard of what "stupid" behavior is; it varies from person to person and from group to group. In order to never ever look stupid, that is, to never do anything that anyone in the world would ever disapprove of, you would have to restrict your behavior to an unhealthy degree. And who knows, maybe like the emperor, you might even be manipulated into doing

26

something that is not in your best interests.

There are many swindlers in this world who know this principle all too well, and use it to marvelous effect. They constantly try to manipulate your actions, not with logical direct arguments, but instead by implying "if you don't do this (or buy that), other people will think you are stupid."

The Principles of Applied Stupidity will allow you to overcome your irrational fear of this vaguely defined monster of the mind. Once you discover that these insidious implications are really just cowardly attacks meant to threaten, frighten, or control you, and they have nothing to do with your innate mental abilities, this verbal boogeyman will no longer have the power to limit or control your actions.

Once you start to recognize and see through these subtle manipulative insinuations, you will no longer be constrained from doing something fun or adventurous, or maybe just a little different, just because someone somewhere has labeled it as being "stupid."

*   *   *

Congratulations! You're half way through the toughest part! Hang in there, it's all downhill from here!

Principle #6:
Everyone Wants to Look and Feel Smart.

We all like to be liked, appreciated, admired, and socially accepted.

We tend to think that we are liked and accepted because we are "smart." Being "smart" represents an ideal status of deserving general social approval (from our teachers anyway). Because we are all trained to associate smartness with social acceptance, everyone wants to be thought of as being smart.

However, this assumption is nonsensical on its face. The smartest kids are social pariahs. Who wants to be seen with a geek or a nerd? They're brilliant, but they're not *smart*.

The whole concept of "smart" is what other people find to be appealing. Everyone wants acceptance and approval from their peers and authority figures, and getting that approval means being conveniently smack dab in the middle of the intellectual bell curve, not below it ... or *above* it. Being called "smart" is a figurative cookie designed to reward you for conforming to the rules, and thereby making your supervisor's life easier.

Subjective opinions of your overall behavior and social acceptability are one thing. Your actual brainpower is something else altogether. The Principles of Applied Stupidity are all about understanding these differences, and not letting the words "smart" and "stupid" have any power over you.

Principle #7:
Stupidity and Ignorance Are Infinite.

Smartist dogma has probably taught you that stupidity and ignorance are always bad, so the above Principle may sound like a rather cynical statement of infinite badness. But here is a different way of looking at it:

If you were to sit down and somehow write down all the knowledge you possess, and who knows, while you're at it, maybe even write down all the knowledge possessed by everyone else in the world, well, no doubt you would write a very long book . . . but you would eventually finish it. This is because everything we currently know and understand as of today has an endpoint. In other words, what we know and understand as of today exists in a finite amount. True, it is constantly expanding here and there, but at any given moment, it has an endpoint.

On the other hand, what you don't know and what you don't understand are infinite. There is no limit to what you, or even Einstein, did *not* know.

Therefore, the greatest possibilities for your future do not lie within the limited finite realm what you currently know and understand. They lie within the infinite domain of what you *don't* currently know or understand. In other words, the greatest possibilities for your future lie within the realm of . . . stupidity.

Principle #8:
There Is Nothing Wrong with Being Stupid.

Associating feelings of shame and inadequacy with your not possessing specific bits of information is not natural. In fact, it is completely contrived. Newborn babies know absolutely nothing, but this doesn't make them feel any less valuable. They have to be taught to associate shame and negativity with their intrinsic natural, neophyte, open-minded selves.

It makes no sense to feel ashamed of not knowing something. Every new project, every new growth, and every new adventure begins with a form of stupidity; that is, a mental state of not knowing the answer or what to expect. Stupidity (that is to say, passing through a phase of becoming aware of your ignorance) is essential to growth, happiness, and any meaningful enterprise.

When you take the collective knowledge and brain power of the human race and compare it what we do NOT know about the universe, we are all, in a sense, idiots. There is nothing wrong with that. Embracing stupidity means being honest about who you are. It means being aware of the fact that we can always learn more. This is the first step towards greater wisdom and enlightenment.

Principle #9:
Knowledge Is Often Counterproductive.

While knowledge has many uses and benefits, knowledge is not universally effective, nor is possession of it always the best route to success.

For one thing, if you already "know everything," you are less likely to be open to new ideas. Second, a great of deal of what is called "knowledge" is really just awareness of a collective experience of failure. If a number of people try to do something and fail, well, being human, instead of blaming themselves, they often rationalize their failure by blaming the "impossibility" of the task. Eventually, this collective belief becomes "knowledge." If you "know," for example, that it's impossible to run a four minute mile, put a man on the moon, or break the sound barrier, you will never try to do such things. Trying to do impossible things is, of course, a pointless waste of time and energy, therefore such attempts are considered to be "stupid."

On the other hand, if you are blissfully unaware that something is impossible, you are far more likely to attempt it. Who knows? Sure, you'll probably fail, but at least you will have a shot at succeeding. An intelligent person has no chance at all, as they believe there is no point in trying. Even if they do try, they will actually be motivated to fail, as they will be disposed, even eager, to confirm their pre-existing belief in the impossibility of the task.

And now, the final Basic Principle . . .

Principle #10:
Embrace Your Inner Idiot.

We live in a "smartist" society. The smartist world view maintains a strict dogma, which is:

"All things smart and intelligent are good . . .
          . . . and all things 'stupid' are bad."

Smartist dogma leads us directly to Principles #5 and #6, i.e., we generally suffer from a fear of looking stupid, and we are often dogged by a need to always look smart. Principle #10 allows you to easily and effectively combat these forces, and gives control of your life back to you.

"Smartist" culture is not benign. It is based on a panicked notion that there is something inherently wrong with you. It says that your natural state is somehow wrong, and so it must be fixed, taught, indoctrinated, changed, conformed, enlightened, and disciplined.

Granted, there is much that is useful to know, and there is certainly nothing wrong with trying to improve yourself. But it's also important to accept and value your intrinsic "as-is" self as well, warts and all.

Principle #10 is based on the idea that you are a decent person as is, and the real answer to life's challenges is to embrace and develop that inherent unique goodness.

Utilizing this principle will not mean you are actually stupid. You could not lessen your actual IQ even if you tried. "Inner idiot" is just a handy catch-all term for all the many imperfections and unique attributes you possess.

Once you start to accept and embrace your inner idiot, all sorts of artificial pressures (to look smart) and limitations (to avoid looking dumb) will disappear. You will step off a psychological hamster wheel, and you will start to take greater control of your life. Once you decide that it doesn't matter whether anyone thinks of you as being smart or dumb, you are free. All sorts of previously impossible or taboo activities will become possible for you to do.

By applying this one simple principle, forgiveness is yours at every turn, no matter what you mess up. You will fly free of a dysfunctional system of conditional love that was installed in your subconscious in grade school for the purpose of manipulating you and making you behave and conform.

Even though this principle is fairly simple, implementing it is not always easy. There is a lifetime of "you-must-not-ever-look-stupid" paranoia and "you-must-always-look-smart" pressure that you will have to overcome. In the following pages, you will discover the many ways to apply this principle, and you will also see the many advantages that can be gained by embracing your inner idiot.

One immediate benefit: strange though this may seem, once you choose to no longer disapprove of your "stupidity," much of what you currently call your "stupidity" will simply disappear. Fact is, it never really existed. The word "stupidity" is an expression of disapproval, and if you *approve* of your stupidity, well, like adding a positive and negative of the same number, the two ideas cancel each other out.

Another benefit, and granted, this is truly odd: the less smart you try to be, the smarter other people will think you are.

33

Part Three:

Advanced Principles of Applied Stupidity

Congratulations! You have made it through the toughest part of the book. Now that you know the Basic Principles of Applied Stupidity, you are ready to put these principles to work in real world situations.

The overall idea here is not to actually become "stupid." That would be impossible. The following chapters are intended to show you how to merely *emulate* stupidity (i.e., a state of not thinking and/or not knowing) when circumstances demand it. This will, in most cases, gain the same wonderful result as actual stupidity.

This is incredibly easy to do. The beauty of it is, it always consists of thinking less, knowing less, and/or doing less . . . or even doing nothing at all. In fact, since there is so little to it, and it's so simple and easy to do, a great deal of the book is simply about giving yourself permission to do it, rather than *how* you should do it.

Very soon you will find many things coming together with virtually no effort, as you will be letting the "smart" people do all the work. No one will question your emulated stupidity, either; most people are terribly eager to look and feel smart (Principle #6), so they are wonderfully willing to believe that someone else is dumber than they are.

Just FYI, the following Advanced Principles begin with workplace and professional environments, then we will move on to personal and artistic endeavors. Let us begin with . . .

Stupidity and Management Part I

The typical standard management model of most organizations is based on the theory that the person in charge is the smartest person in the organization. This is an easy assumption to make. After all, the boss/manager usually has a college degree and all the other trappings of being more intelligent than everyone else. We tend to automatically accept the idea that their greater "smartness" is why they are in charge and why they make more money.

But here is the problem: if the person at the top of the management ladder is seen as the smartest person in the organization, this immediately implies that the people who report to that person are not as smart. And if it is a multi-layered organization, then each succeeding lower layer of the hierarchy is obliged to do less and less independent thinking, or, if you will excuse the colloquial phraseology, to be and to act dumber and dumber than the layer above, with each lower layer of worker totally deferring to all instructions from upper layers.

If you were to create a graphic to illustrate this system, you would end up with an inverted pyramid. In this inverted pyramid, all the intelligence is at the top. As the requirement to be less and less intelligent cascades down through the ranks, when you finally get to the bottom, you will see a most interesting effect: all the people at the bottom (i.e., the ones who are on the assembly line actually making the product, or the ones who are interacting directly with customers), are required to suppress all independent thinking. In many cases these "lower-downs" have just as much (or more) knowledge, intelligence, or experience as the management, but they are not allowed to use it. In other words, from the point of view of the customer, these lower-level "associates" are totally stupid, in the sense that they are unresponsive and/or uncommunicative. Simple common sense is consistently trumped by "policy." If you happen to be the unhappy customer facing such a situation, no amount of complaining will change anything, as these lower-level employees are not allowed to be or to do anything else.

This oh-so-common management model is a direct result of Principle #6 (Everyone Wants to Look and Feel Smart). In this case, the person with the most power uses that power to indulge their own need to look smart, by requiring the people under their control to be functionally stupid.

While it is certainly tempting to indulge one's desire to be the smartest person in the company, to maximize one's effectiveness as a manager, it would be far better to utilize Principle #1 (i.e., The Absence of Thought and Information Is Just as Powerful as the Presence of Thought and Information). To apply this Principle in a management situation, we use:

Principle #11:
The Less Thinking a Manager Does,
the More Thinking the People
Who Work for That Manager
Have to Do, and Vice Versa.

For a manager to be truly effective and get the most and best performance out of his or her subordinates, it is essential for that manager to be as dumb as possible. That way, employees will no longer spend 90% of their time and energy avoiding doing anything bright or creative that might make accidentally make that boss (or any other managers) feel stupid. Instead, with the management's incompetence and confusion now openly acknowledged, those same formerly unmotivated "dumb" employees will now be forced to tap into their own intellect and

37

imagination, and work at their highest efficiency. They must do so in order to fill the endless infinite void of the management's mental non-activity.

Stupidity and Management Part II

While a mental vacuum is a powerful management tool all by itself, management is of course a complicated activity. Doing it well involves the use of several Principles of Applied Stupidity all at the same time. In order for the above Principle #11 to work, again, a manager must be able to refrain from being unduly influenced by Principle #6 (Everyone Wants to Look and Feel Smart). However, along with that, a manager must *also* be mindful of the universal power of Principle #5 (Fear of Looking Stupid Is an Enormous Force).

Here is how this works: In a standard employee-to-manager relationship, the typical employee is always going to assume that Principle #5 (Fear of Looking Stupid Is an Enormous Force) is having its usual full effect upon their manager (or anyone else in a position of power over them). Therefore, employees always assume that deferring to a manager's need to feel smart is necessary to maintain job security. This means that employees will never risk doing anything that might make a boss or manager feel stupid. This translates to their never contradicting orders, never pointing out a boss's errors, and never offering any truly new ideas or meaningful suggestions.

Standard employee survival instinct will always default to the safe mode of never challenging their manager's intelligence. Therefore, for a manager to be truly effective, they have to somehow override this default self-protective smartist presumption on the part of their employees. The Principles of Applied Stupidity make this easy to do. In this case, to achieve this change, one should openly apply Principle #10 (Embrace Your Inner Idiot).

If a manager openly states that he/she has no idea what they are doing, there is no longer a need by the employees to adroitly avoid doing anything that might make that manager feel stupid, as the boss's stupidity (already assumed) is now openly acknowledged. This creates an environment where a much freer and more open exchange of ideas is immediately established.

Stupidity and Management Part III

Removing your employees' fear of offending you is a lot like taking your foot off the brakes. In the next step, you can go one step further, and step on the gas.

Once you have removed your employees' fear of the negative consequences that would result from their being openly cleverer and more productive than yourself, the next step is all about using Principle #6 (Everyone Wants to Look and Feel Smart) to marvelous advantage.

One of the things that really motivates people is having a chance to show off how smart they are. It's astonishing what people will do to get recognized in this way.

This is a wonderfully handy, ready-made management tool. However, when most managers try to use it, it doesn't work for them, because they skip the necessary first step of admitting to their own stupidity. It is always fascinating to see some managers endlessly looking for ways to "motivate" their employees. They keep stepping on the gas pedal, but they never take their foot off the brakes, i.e., they don't remove the penalties that will be visited upon the employees if they ever dare to even come close to displaying greater intelligence or greater knowledge than the boss.

Only when it's safe to do so, i.e., when the power of Principle #5 is removed (in this case we are talking about the boss's fear of looking stupid, not the employees' fear), will employees let themselves be motivated by Principle #6 (Everyone Wants to Look and Feel Smart) and allow themselves to indulge in the pleasurable opportunity to look smarter than the boss. But again, the only way this can occur is if the boss is willing to be openly seen as being "less smart." If a manager wants to make this happen, they must be very proactive in making use of the Principles of Applied Stupidity. Otherwise the default (inverted pyramid) management system of cascading dumbness will manifest itself without mercy.

If you are a manager, you have nothing to lose by using this approach. As previously mentioned, most employees already think their boss is an idiot anyway. You may as well take advantage of that, and let them "help you" to achieve ever greater profits and bonuses. And by the way, the dumber you look, the more "compensation" people will think you need in order to simply survive.

Stupidity and "Back-Management" (IV)

Now of course some of you may be saying, "That would be great information to use if I were the manager, but I'm the guy being managed by an idiot who thinks he's smart. He has all the power. What do I do?"

Well that's a good question, and it applies to an awful lot of people. If you are in the aforementioned situation, you have three choices: 1) you can quit 2) you can hunker down and take the pain, or 3) you can use the Principles of Applied Stupidity to solve the problem. Unlike knowledge or intelligence, stupidity is infinite, and can therefore be used to manage virtually any situation.

If you are in conflict with a boss or manager that is trapped in the grip of smartism, well, you have a problem. They always have to be the smart one, and they never listen to you or try anything new. But at the same time, here is your grand opportunity.

It's fairly safe to say that this person is a little short on external smartness strokes. In other words, no one ever tells them they are smart; instead they are constantly being told, subtly or not so subtly, both by employees like yourself, as well as by his/her own bosses, that you all think he/she is an idiot.

To deal with this oh-so-common situation, you must first accept the annoying fact that trying to convince this person that you are smarter than they are will never work. (Okay, it *might* work, but that would require a grand epiphany of both brilliant insight and deep humility on their part, and in case you haven't noticed, grand epiphanies of brilliant insight and deep humility have been in short supply for some time now. This "intelligent" confrontational approach will more than likely only garner increased resistance to anything you have to say.)

Instead of fighting the smartism, why not tap into the infinite power of stupidity to manage the situation? In this case, by embracing your inner idiot, you can easily become the #1 source of smartness praise for this manager. It does not matter how dumb they are; stupidity is infinite, therefore it is always possible for you to be dumber. Don't say anything about what they do wrong. Endlessly praise and admire what they do right (if you can't find anything, well, just tell them they are smart generally). Eventually, since you are the only person who is telling them something they want to hear, i.e., that they are smart, that manager might actually begin to listen to what you have to say. At that point, you can start to initiate change and growth.

Results are not guaranteed, but this approach is still way better than making them feel stupid from the get-go, which is pretty much guaranteed to fail.

Resisting stupidity is pointless, as you will discover in a future chapter. Make it your ally. Instead of subtly implying to this manager/boss that you think they are really dumb, out-do their brainlessness by tapping in to your own infinite internal reservoir of stupidity. Once they get hooked on feeling smarter than you are, you can simply tell them (euphemizing it of course to suit your situation): "As smart as you already are, you would be even smarter if you were to do (whatever it is *you* want done)."

Now of course, at first glance, this probably strikes you as being humiliating and degrading and a huge waste of time, but you wouldn't be reading this if you weren't desperate. Don't let your own smartist prejudices stop you from using an extremely effective tool. Many people are caught up in a trap of smartism. Every year, billions of tax dollars are spent on training people to unquestioningly believe that smart is always good and stupid is always bad. Why not use that training for your own purposes? Stupidity is power.

(Note, as a general guideline, when training an insecure person to listen to you, ten compliments per each piece of constructive criticism is a good ratio to start with.)

Stupidity and Management Part V

Orchestral conductors are often used as a metaphor for management. Sounds good on paper, but all orchestral conductors are not created equal. Some, of course, are great; most, including some with considerable musical talent, are obscure. So what makes the difference?

There are many things that will make one conductor stand out from their massive competition, but one of the skills that all of the great conductors have is the use of the Principles of Applied Stupidity. How does this work? Well . . .

Contrary to popular belief, the conductor's task is not to control the players. Orchestras are actually the ultimate team sport. The conductor's job is to maximize the team's focus and energy.

For example, at the very beginning of a piece of music, 90 people all have to come in at the exact same instant, and then continue to play each note within milliseconds of each other throughout the concert. The extraordinary rhythmic unity—conformity, if you will—of the ensemble is one of the many technical things that makes a great orchestra "great." But while that extreme conformity is part of the "greatness" of the orchestra, the "greatness" of the conductor does not come from his inspiring even higher levels of unity and conformity. The orchestra can achieve that conformity on its own, as can any cheap computer music program. What the orchestra needs, in addition to its inherent conformity (i.e., "intelligence") is a leader who departs from this "intelligence" and takes the orchestra out of its safety zone of default total unity. Doing this requires a willingness to do something *different.* In other words, leading a great orchestra requires the willingness to risk being thought "dumb" (that is to say, to risk getting disapproval for departing from the norm) . . . and in my own experience of working as a bass player, only a small minority of conductors were willing to do that. It was amazing to see just how many conductors believed that their job description was to maintain order, achieve total control, demand total obedience, repress anything unusual or unexpected or out of the ordinary, and make it sound "just like the record."

Yes, it is important for a leader to give the team a clear goal, but in an orchestra, the composer has already done that. In the context of a major orchestra, the conductor has a choice: does he/she get out of the way, defer to the higher collective knowledge of the players, let some of the most skilled artists on the planet meld their minds and souls together, and, guided by tradition, team spirit, and the sonic choreography of a master composer, allow the full potential of the musical magic to happen? Or does the conductor limit the overall flow of energy and information to a much lower level of dull performance, which conforms to some codified standard, bores the audience to death, and only serves to give the conductor a feeling of being in total control?

It is truly astonishing just how many people think that the latter is leadership. They are so steeped in the dogma of smartism that they cannot conceive of any other way.

The real difference in the great ones is that they appreciate the collective knowledge of the players, and they accept that they cannot match it. So they don't compete. Instead, they do the one thing that they *can* do as an individual to match the collective energy of the orchestra, which is to present a massive infinite vacuum of open-minded listening. In other words, the great conductors use the power of Applied Stupidity. In response, the players of the orchestra are compelled to dig deep

47

into their own internal reservoirs of musical ability to fill that vacuum. No matter how much information or knowledge the players generate, it can never fill the infinite vacuum of a great conductor's stupidity. The best conductors were famous for doing less and less, as this consistently required the players to do more and more.

The *removal* of many managerial processes (such as demands for strict compliance with specific top-down instruction) generally inspires much greater effort and teamwork. You can see this happening yourself at intersections with broken traffic lights. Have you ever noticed that, when the power goes out and traffic lights don't work, even at the busiest intersections, there is never much of a buildup or delay in traffic flow? True, more thought is demanded from individual drivers, and maybe it's not quite as safe, but everyone ultimately moves faster and is forced, by lack of authority and direction from above, to work more cooperatively.

Conversely, the centralized control of overzealous leaders (who need to constantly demonstrate to their teams how smart they are) always bogs everything down. Cops directing traffic generally have the same effect.

To be honest, a lot of orchestral musicians actually prefer traffic cops and the lesser conductors, because with those kinds of leaders, all you have to do is turn off your brain and follow along. Everything is on autopilot, someone else tells you what to do, and life is simple and easy. Boring, but easy. Great conductors, on the other hand, make you work at the highest levels of your own potential. This is exciting, but it's also kind of scary.

Stupidity and Management Part VI

Speaking of Conductors . . .

Arthur Fiedler was arguably the most famous and successful conductor ever. So here is a question: with so many people out there wanting to be famous conductors of big orchestras, how is it that Arthur managed to outdistance them all? After all, he was certainly not the greatest musician in the world; in terms of musical talent, he was average in almost every way. From a smartist viewpoint, his success makes no sense at all. However, his massive success *does* make sense in light of his use of the Principles of Applied Stupidity.

If you look at conductors the world over, you will see that, while they are usually very "smart" (as defined in terms of their schoolwork and such), their intense training makes them pretty much all look alike. They are all wearing white ties and tails. Now it is true that some of them allow themselves to be photographed in dramatic poses that, generally speaking, look like a freeze frame of a knife fight. But even in these pictures (that are meant to imply extreme individual emotional intensity), they all start to look the same after a while.

The reason why Arthur Fiedler became so popular was very simple: he was able to distinguish himself from the rest of the herd by the simple fact that he was willing to risk "looking stupid," i.e., he was willing to be different, and do things that the musical establishment consistently said were obviously "wrong." Conformity dogs the music business at every turn, and it seems conductors are tripping over each other trying to conform more and more to the centralized stereotype of what a conductor should look like. Granted, this conformed approach has one big advantage: there is little chance of having the disapproval experience of being told you "look stupid" if you look exactly how people expect you to look. Arthur understood the power of looking stupid, and never followed such narrow rules.

If you ever look at some old Boston Pops record covers, you will see Arthur in all sorts of unusual outfits: either wild west garb, or a George M. Cohan Stars and Stripes suit, a movie director outfit complete with riding pants, beret, and megaphone, or even in a big floppy Pagliacci clown suit.

Doing something different or "unfamiliar" is a common definition of "looking stupid." Arthur was not afraid of doing different things. Along with these unusual costumes and poses on the covers of his recordings, he also made highly unusual programming choices. He had many programming ideas that people trained in the culture of classical music all condemned as "stupid," i.e., something that is not known to be universally acceptable. For example, he commissioned orchestral arrangements of Beatles hits. These arrangements required the players in the orchestra to occasionally sing "Yeah, yeah, yeah." The musicians in the orchestra hated doing this, as it made them "feel stupid." Even though many people in the music industry told Arthur that these were all stupid ideas (meaning they were untried and not guaranteed to work, and might be embarrassing in any case). Arthur ignored them. These wacky ideas worked beautifully. The crowds loved them.

Arthur allowed all sorts of crazy things to go on at Pops concerts. There was one piece called *Pops Hoedown* that contained various barnyard tunes (e.g., *Turkey in the Straw*). Strange as this may seem, a Pops performance of this piece would include one of the first violinists standing up (about half way through) with an actual 12-gage shotgun. On cue, this violinist would pretend to shoot at a rubber chicken that had been tossed in the air by someone in the percussion section. Stupid? Silly? Ridiculous? Of course. And the audience ate it up.

However, lest you think it was all shlock and no substance, consider this: in 1976, half a million people showed up for Arthur's Bicentennial concert. The first half of the program was the entire Tchaikovsky *B-flat Piano Concerto*. Anyone with any common sense will tell you that a 40-minute piano concerto couldn't possibly maintain the interest of a rowdy gathering of 500,000 people who came mostly for the fireworks, but amazingly, it did.

Orchestras are very staid and traditional enterprises, and so Arthur's many departures from the norm—all of which, taken together, were key to his success—were each derided at their inception by many people as being "stupid." Arthur paid no attention to them. His willingness to take an unconventional approach to everything he did—in other words, consistently accepting the risk of "looking stupid"—was, more than any other single factor, the key to his success.

If you ever get hired to do the gig, here is a little advice: it's not all that hard to throw a rubber chicken up in the air in Symphony Hall. What's hard is overcoming your fear of looking stupid just before you do it.

The ability to overcome the fear of being seen as "different" (i.e., stupid) is the key to innovation. Overcoming that fear, far more than "having talent," is the one of the most essential elements of success in any creative or competitive enterprise.

"I am looking for a lot of men who have an infinite capacity to not know what can't be done."
−Henry Ford

Stupidity and Management Part VII: Management and Too-Smart Employees

Just as "needing to always look smart" is a tremendous disadvantage to a person in a management position, having employees who want to be seen as smart can be a problem as well. We often talk about wanting the smartest people we can get as employees, but standard "intelligence" is often in direct conflict with many desirable employee attributes, especially initiative.

The people who did well in school generally did so because they eagerly waited for assignments, and when they got them, they did them perfectly. They were immensely rewarded for this behavior over and over again, until a homework assignment made them salivate like Pavlov's dogs (there is a joke in here somewhere about Pavlov's dogs salivating just before eating his homework, but I can't find it). This is great for the symbiotic relationship between teachers and their gifted kids, but when these gifted kids grow up and get jobs, nothing changes; they eagerly and endlessly wait for assignments, and when they get them, they attempt to achieve perfection on the very first try. Their primary goal is to again receive the delicious longed-for affirmation and praise from the boss/teacher by getting an A+ or a "100."

This is great as far as it goes, but such people, brilliant though they may be, are handicapped by this training. Very often, 1) they are generally unable to start a project on their own, as they are used to always being told what to do and 2) whatever project they set out to do is either severely limited in scope or never gets finished, because they have been taught to always seek perfection in their work. They have no other reference or purpose, as all of their output for sixteen years (or more) was designed for one single type of "buyer persona," i.e., a teacher.

Unlike curricula and tests, life and the marketplace seldom offer perfectly planned structure, nor do they offer a perfect score for much of anything. And so when the goal becomes perfection, the task simply doesn't get done, or it takes so long to do it that it becomes economically unsustainable.

Many managers encounter this problem. They hire brilliant underlings and assistants, and they assume academic brilliance will translate into initiative, but very often it doesn't. All too often, these brilliant assistants consistently wait and wait for instructions to act. When asked to be creative, they research and imitate. When they are given something simple to do, they don't just do the quick and dirty minimum and then come back for the next assignment. Instead, they spend the entire day designing a custom font for the address label of an envelope that is going to the gas company.

Many managers get confused in this situation. They cannot understand how employees that are supposed to be so smart can be so stupid. Fortunately, the situation can be rectified if one understands the Principles of Applied Stupidity.

In this case, the employees in question are "stupid" only in the sense that they are doing things that you disapprove of. The real problem is not a *lack* of intelligence. The problem is actually a *surplus* of intelligence. The problem is the general eagerness to do things in a "smart" way, i.e., the same way they were taught to do things in school. Recognizing the true nature of the problem is the first step in solving it. In this case, the solution is not to make them more smart; the solution is to somehow make them *less* smart.

Of course, the easiest way to deal with this problem is to hire C students in the first place. They are much more likely to understand and embrace the philosophy of just doing a passable job, and then quickly moving on to more important things.

If the previous paragraph is too little too late, well, you have a few options. You can: 1) create hiring policies that garner less intelligent employees, who will be more efficient and effective, if somewhat harder to control; 2) take a look at yourself and see if you are rewarding and encouraging this behavior; and 3) take an even harder look at yourself and see if you are being "played" by people who are letting you think you are smarter than they are.

Your last and best option though, is a permutation of Principle #11 (The less a Manager Does, the More the Workers Have to Do.). As previously stated, the joy and wonder of the Principles of Applied Stupidity is how they allow you to get and do more by thinking, doing, working, and knowing less. In this case, you have people who have a lot of potential, but they have been trained to be obedient. Obedient minions are a tremendous temptation, but the less you do, the less you say, and the less of your own authority you give them to obey, the more they will have to think and act on their own.

"You must unlearn what you have learned."
                                    –Jedi Master Yoda

Stupidity and Information

The purpose of this book is not to say that you should give up using your intelligence, nor is it to recommend that you endeavor to be as stupid as you possibly can all the time. What intelligence you do have should be used to its furthest limit. The purpose of this book is simply to point out to you that you don't have to stop there. Your intelligence is fine as far as it goes, but in addition to what you know, what you don't know or understand exists in infinite amounts. This is true of you and of everyone else. Such things are nothing to be ashamed of, and when you combine what you know with what you don't know, they can be far more effective that the mere application of what you know all by itself.

Here is an excellent example:

You are probably familiar with phrases extolling the virtues of knowledge and information, such as "information is power." It is generally true, no matter how smart or how stupid you may be, those people who have more information generally have an advantage over those of us who have no idea what is going on. One definition of being "intelligent" is being educated, or, more specifically, possessing more information. So, one would normally think that being intelligent would lead to constantly acquiring even more information. While that may be true in some cases, generally speaking, the opposite is more likely to be the case; stupidity is far more helpful in acquiring new and useful information. This is due to

Principle #12:
Information Flows from Smart to Dumb.

Information is a kind of energy. While it is occasionally captured in printed form, for the most part, information exists as electrical synapses in the mind. Therefore, information functions very much like other forms of energy.

If you think of information energy as a kind of electrical energy, then you can envision it flowing. Generally speaking, energy flows from where it is . . . to where it isn't. For example, electricity flows *from* a power plant . . . *to* your house. In another example, clouds store up a charge of electricity, but the electricity flows out from the cloud only when it gets near enough to a tree and has a place to put it. It goes from where it is (the cloud) to where it isn't (the tree).

If there is no place for the electrical energy to go, it just sits in the cloud and does nothing. It is, literally, static. Other examples: the energy doesn't flow out of a battery until you connect it to something. The hair dryer doesn't electrocute you until you throw it into your bathtub. In all these examples, the energy doesn't flow unless it has a place to go.

Just as electrical energy flows from outlets to your appliances, informational energy flows in exactly the same way. It flows from where it is . . . to where it isn't. If one person has information and another person does not, that information can only flow in one direction. It flows from where it is to where it isn't.

Here is where the smartist training you may have received—i.e., to always exhibit as much intelligence as possible—may not be such a good idea. When two smart people get in a room together, information does not flow easily. Due to the constant effect of Principle #5 (Fear of Looking Stupid Is an Enormous Force), neither person wants to admit that the other person is smarter than they are. This results in neither person listening to the other. It's not that the information energy isn't there; it's just that it is being mutually repelled. You see this all the time on those faux-news TV shows where two people, each representing the extreme opposite end of a given issue, bark out their opinions. They don't listen to the other person at all. Entertaining in a weird sort of way, but no information is really being exchanged between them. The information is actually being mutually repelled, like when you try to put the positive poles of two magnets together.

Now consider the same room, but instead of two smart people, you have one smart person . . . and one *dumb* person. The smart person now has a place for his/her information energy to go. The presence of a dumb person gives them a wonderful platform for showing off their knowledge. In keeping with Principle #6 (Everyone Wants to Look and Feel Smart), this is an irresistible opportunity. The smart person talks and talks, and the dumb person just looks intrigued and takes in all that free information.

Unfortunately, even though the best way to receive new and useful information is to emulate a state of stupidity, we often let our smartist training interrupt the flow of intelligence to us. Our eagerness to look smart makes us resistant to new information. We don't want to accept new information, no matter how useful it may be, because its very existence means we didn't know as much as we thought we did. Principle #5 (Fear of Looking Stupid Is an Enormous Force) makes us want to shut out new information. Even if you aren't actively resisting new information, if you appear to be smart, no one will tell you anything, simply because they will assume that, being so smart, you know it already. Again, Principle #5 is at work, and they don't want to risk looking stupid by telling you something you may already know.

If you are the smartest person in a room, good for you, but it is still quite possible that one of the relatively less intelligent people in the room may have some small piece of information that will benefit you. If you look too smart, that information will not flow to you. By emulating greater stupidity, you will create greater access to more and more useful information.

Admittedly, this is not a perfect system. There are many people who have rather uninteresting or redundant information that they are constantly trying to share with anyone and everyone (usually in a vain attempt to look smart). However, at the same time, there also may be someone in the room who possesses very useful information, and it's hard to tell in advance of hearing it just who has the useful information and who doesn't. The only way you can find out is if you have access to all of it, good and bad. If you want information to flow to you, you must not resist it by constantly demonstrating how smart you are. Instead of expending energy on maintaining a smart appearance, it is far better (and so much easier) to just relax, and look and act stupid. If you do this, everyone else will feel delightfully superior to you, and this will impel them to share all of their knowledge with you.

It may take some effort for you to overcome the pointless distaste you may have for being perceived as dumb, but once you do, you will become a lightning rod for information. People will enjoy your presence because they are assured of not feeling put down. They will all indulge themselves in looking smart by imparting all of their information to you. If you let this go on long enough, pretty soon you will know everything that everyone else knows. At that point you will of course also know what *you* know, and when you add it all together, you will have more information. In other words, by appearing to be dumb, you will eventually become smarter than everyone else.

Overcoming Your Resistance to
Being Thought Dumb

Despite the many obvious benefits of the Principles of Applied Stupidity, you may have trouble taking advantage of them because, like most people, you probably have a fear of being called or considered "dumb." After all, when you were growing up, this was a fear you had to live with every day. No one wants to risk re-living the horrors of grade school, where our teachers used our pubescent anxiety and self-consciousness as a way of maintaining control over a bunch of little hormone-crazed monsters. To help you overcome these pernicious fears lying deep within your subconscious, we suggest that you consider the extraordinary benefits to be gained by implementing the next Principle of Applied Stupidity, which is

Principle #13:
Letting People Feel Smarter than You
Makes You Look Even Smarter to Them.

This Principle may seem self-contradictory, but here is what happens when you apply this principle: When you allow other people to "feel smart," what you are really doing is offering them the social acceptance they are so eagerly and desperately seeking. Granted, it would be easy to assume that letting people beat you at some sort of abstract intellectual competition would make them feel contempt for you. After all, smartist training says smart people are "better" than dumb people. But since we are talking about emotion, when you let other people feel "smart," you are really making them feel good, as you are meeting their innermost emotional needs. Since you are doing that, in their minds, you will appear to be a genius. They will eventually jump through any hoop you set for them, if you just promise them another "smartness recognition" cookie for doing so.

To illustrate how this works, let's suppose you are working for a manager who is quite brilliant, but only says something to you when you make a mistake. In such a circumstance, you have no choice but to focus your mind on avoiding mistakes. Your work becomes perfect, but highly limited. Doing more work creates ever greater possibility of error, so the less work you do, the better. No matter how smart this boss may be on paper, you can't help but see the drop in your own productivity. You will therefore label the boss as being "stupid," defined here as deserving disapproval.

Now let's flip things around, and say you have a manager who appreciates the quality of the work you do. When you present new ideas to him or her, this manager does not immediately compare these ideas to some external pre-existing standard, but instead throws his/her mind open to these new ideas and perceives their potential value.

One could make an argument that, since you are coming up with all these great ideas, you are the "smarter" one. But since this manager is approving of you, you will approve of their management. In the back of your mind, you will find yourself saying, "How unusual it is to meet someone who appreciates my otherwise unappreciated talents. *This manager is a genius*."

The role of manager is not about being a genius and being smarter than all of the managees. The role of a manager is to make all the people he/she manages function like geniuses themselves. The best way to do this is not to compete, but to step aside and let the genius of others flow. This is the just one more instance of the wonderful power and magic of the Principles of Applied Stupidity.

Stupidity and Listening

One of the greatest disservices of smartist culture is the way it makes us feel at odds with our fellow human beings. We are told that we must always strive to be relatively "smarter." Sounds noble enough, but to achieve this nebulous "smarter" status, we often forget that in order for this system to work, i.e., if we are to be "smarter," this means that somehow, somewhere, someone else has to be relatively "dumber." Hidden in all this ambitious idealism is a dark underside, which is a perpetual incentive to ignore or beat down other people's ideas while advancing our own. Winning such conflicts supposedly proves you are somehow smarter, and according to smartist dogma, to be seen as being mentally superior is inherently good, period. Many people subscribe to this system, but consider the following story:

Once upon a time there was a big-time consultant who was hired to make a presentation to the entire management team of a large company. He had been doing this kind of work for many years and was highly regarded in his field. Unfortunately, the person who hired him, a vice president of the company in question, created a problem for the consultant. This company VP was very concerned about the success of the event, and had all sorts of odd suggestions for how this consultant should approach his presentation.

While this consultant was happy to be making a large speaking fee, at the same time he was not terribly thrilled about having this VP call him every day with more suggestions and ideas. This consultant had been giving this kind of talk for years and was known as a foremost expert. Even so, this VP still kept calling with more and more suggestions. While the consultant wanted to maintain a good relationship for purposes of future business, he was getting quite vexed by this client. He found himself feeling ever more frustrated, as he really dreaded these phone calls and endless suggestions.

Finally, since all else had failed, just as an experiment, he tried using the Principles of Applied Stupidity. In this case, he used Principle #10; i.e., this consultant imagined that, instead of being much smarter than his pesky client, he was much dumber.

Well guess what. In imaging himself to be less intelligent than his pesky client, his smartist resistance to new information melted away. Instead of feeling that his "smartness" was being challenged, he viewed each phone call from the client as a help in reducing his "dumbness." This had numerous additional benefits: the client sensed that this big-time consultant was respecting him and telling him how smart he was, which made the VP feel really good about himself (see Principle #6, Everyone Wants to Look and Feel Smart); and, in keeping with Principle #13 (again, Letting People Feel Smarter than You Makes You Look Even Smarter to Them), this also made the VP think this consultant was a genius.

And what was even more amazing, in keeping with principle #2 (Everyone Is a Genius), this consultant discovered (much to his amazement) that this VP actually had some new insight and information that he had never considered before. The experience actually improved his value and service to all of his future clients.

Like so many people, you may also suffer from an acquired resistance to new information, because its very existence implies that you are "stupid." New information inevitably conflicts with your smartist training, i.e., wanting to believe that you have already learned everything. We all like to think that we have "graduated," as that means no one can talk down to us any more. This resistance is a really hard thing to get around, because it is such an ingrained habit of the mind. As long as your goal is simply to attain a state of self-perceived "smartness," you will push assistance away from you. However, if you imagine yourself to be stupid, this will put you in a state of mind where you will feel okay about letting other people help you. Instead of defending your turf, you will be able to import and incorporate a constant stream of new outside ideas, and continually improve yourself.

Principle #14:
Imagining That Other People Are "Smarter" than
You Are Makes You a Better Listener,
and Therefore More Effective in All of Your
Interactions and Communications.

"Lazy people always win. It's like a super power."
—Scott Adams (creator of Dilbert)

Fast-Minded vs. Slow-Minded

One of the common associations we have with intelligence is the concept of faster mental "speed." The ability to "think fast" or be "quick minded" is of course much preferred over the label of being "slow minded." Taking too much time to finish a test or come to a decision is supposedly a sign of shameful stupidity. Therefore, to look smart, and to avoid the possibility of looking stupid, we all endeavor to think as fast as we possibly can.

Again, like so many definitions of smart and stupid, these definitions are based on subjective emotions and vague points of view, not on logical observations or objective criteria.

First of all, it can be argued that thought (any kind of thought; your thought, my thought, an insect's thought) all moves at the same speed. The little synaptic sparks of electricity in your brain aren't moving any faster or slower than the little synaptic sparks of electricity in anyone else's brain. (Incidentally, if you google the phrase "speed of thought," you will get a jillion web pages that collectively say we don't know what it is.)

It's an interesting topic, but the hypothesis that you can a) think faster than someone else, and b) doing so somehow makes you smarter, is very hard to prove, given the fact that we have no idea what the speed of thought actually is.

Even if faster thinking was possible (and who knows, maybe it is), in terms of faster mental speed being an asset generally, well that's yet another interesting blanket assumption of smartist dogma. Consider this question: Let's say you are in a small group of people, perhaps walking down a sidewalk, or maybe taking a tour in a museum. Who determines the pace of the group, the fastest person or the slowest person? Answer: the slowest person.

Another example: If a bunch of mountain climbers are roped together, who determines the pace of the expedition? Again, the pace of the team is determined, not by the fastest member, but by the slowest member. Yes, you can curse that slow member's slowness if you like, and you can express your disapproval by calling them a stupid idiot for going so exasperatingly slow. But no matter—if the group desires to stay together (and most groups do), the slowest member has the power to determine the pace of the group.

A similar situation: Lets say you are driving on a winding, double-yellow median strip two-lane road. How fast can you go? Answer: legally, only as fast as the slowest person ahead of you. Conversely, if you are the slowest one on that same mountain road, you are determining the pace of everyone behind you. This leads us to

Principle #15:
Slowness of Mind, Not Quickness,
Puts You in Charge.

This may strike you as odd. After all, in our society, speed, especially mental speed, is generally thought of as a good thing. Let us dig a little deeper.

Even though high speed thinking is generally thought to be good, high rates of speed in most other endeavors are *not* thought to be good. Haste, hurry, rushing, recklessness . . . these are not positive states of being. In fact, very often, speed implies a state of fear.

Just to give you a few examples of how faster speed is a symptom of fear: most animals move the fastest when they are afraid of getting eaten. When people get nervous, their heart rates speed up, and they talk faster.

Fast thinking, like fast physical movement, is usually an expression of fear. Calm, "slow" thinking is less driven by fear, and since slow thinking is generally more careful and more methodical, it is generally more accurate. Therefore, given its greater accuracy, one could argue that calm, slow thinking is more "intelligent."

One of the main reasons people tell you it is good to be "smart" and to "think fast" is because they don't want you to think too carefully. Instead, they want you to quickly conform to their pace and their way of thinking. How often do we get information that urges us to make a quick decision? "Act now, last one, this is it, going out of business"—? This is often done in an effort to pressure or frighten you into making a snap decision that may not be in your best interests. If you were to think carefully and slowly, you would be less likely to buy certain items. People who want to influence your behavior want you to think less carefully; hence, there is lots of praise and reinforcement for fast thinking, and there is general disapproval of slow, careful thinking.

We curse slow thinkers or slow drivers because they have so much more influence over us than fast ones. A fast driver will drive around you and leave you alone, or they will slow down and adjust to your speed. Either way, they cannot affect your pace. A slow driver, on the other hand, has enormous control. If they are on the road ahead of you, you have to adjust to them.

Speed and intelligence are the ability to adjust. Slowness and stupidity are attributes that force others to adjust to you.

When someone condemns your slow careful thinking, they are probably trying to manipulate your behavior. They are attempting to make you feel ashamed of, and embarrassed by, your true self. If they succeed, they have a better chance of making you abandon your own inner guidance systems and blindly conform to their pace. Again, we discover that the word "stupid" really means shaming disapproval, and this negative energy is often employed to gain a single short term speed-up effect on your behavior. These common attempts at manipulation are easily countered by the application of Principle #10 (i.e., Embracing Your Inner Idiot). Accepting your stupidity frees you from the power of Principle #5 (Fear of Looking Stupid Is an Enormous Force) that overwhelms most people.

When you think fast or drive fast, well, sometimes this is great, but it also raises the likelihood of making an error that could be harmful to you. Dare to be slow. When people scowl at you and tell you that you are thinking too slowly for their taste, take it as a compliment. It doesn't mean you are stupid. It means you are being responsible to yourself. It means you are not letting them control you, intimidate you, or boss you around. It means you are commanding the pace of yourself and of the group, and you are not letting fear rule your thinking.

*   *   *

Question:

What two things do the following four people all have in
common?

Bill Gates
Paul Allen
Michael Dell
Larry Ellison

Answer:

1) They are all on the list of the five richest people in America
and

2) They are all college dropouts.

Fast-Minded Management

Some people believe that a heightened rate of speed in a workplace is an intrinsically good idea. Certainly, in a factory setting, the faster the machines go the better . . . But with people, it's not so clear cut. Granted, heightened unnatural degrees of speed certainly create observable flurries of activity, and these give a very satisfying appearance of an immediate rise in productivity. However, this approach has some rather obvious flaws.

First of all, work done hurriedly is usually full of errors and has to be done over. Therefore, in terms of actual productivity, in the long run, working faster is actually slower.

Second, such hurry-up managerial techniques are generally ineffective, because employees quickly discover there is no point to them; employees know that the moment they move any faster, their new faster pace becomes the baseline that the manager is now required to move them faster than. Employees are therefore motivated to set their baseline speed as slow as possible—even slower than their own preferred pace. They have to do this in order to survive; if they did not resist, and instead allowed this constant-acceleration managerial philosophy to be taken to its logical theoretical conclusion, they and their co-workers would eventually burn up in a fireball caused by the friction of the air as they career toward the copy machine at 24,000 miles per hour.

Pressuring people to "hurry up" may look like greater efficiency or control, but moving faster simply for the sake of moving faster is, again, really just an expression of fear–and it's a ridiculous fear, too. It's a fear that our natural rhythm, i.e., what we intrinsically are, is somehow not good enough. Smartist dogma demands that we move faster and faster in order to somehow to create an illusion of being "smarter" than what we really are. It serves no real purpose.

Also, the use of fear as a motivation for faster speed in the workplace always has consequences to pay down the road: burnout, stress-induced illness and downtime, plus high turnover and the attendant costs of rehiring and retraining, just to name a few.

Moving quickly or thinking quickly is, evolutionarily speaking, supposed to be a short term stopgap measure to get you away from danger, not to be a way of life. In other words, unless you are being chased by a tiger, moving as fast as you can makes no sense. To never slow down to your own healthy pace of existence is, in terms of the quality of the reasoning supporting the decision, *stupid*, in that it deserves to be condemned as a poor choice. It fails to make full use of your greatest potential, as that can only be attained when you are not frantic and instead working at a sensible natural pace.

Managers who pressure you to constantly do things faster and faster may achieve some short term gains in productivity at first, but such managers, like the people who tailgate you on a mountain road, eventually become powerless and despised.

Here is the question one should ask about such a manager: Is there in fact a specific speed which, if reached, would make that manager happy? And if reached, is that high rate of speed really the optimum long-term pace for overall efficiency and communication? Or . . . does this manager just have a never-ending need for everyone to go faster than whatever speed you are currently going?

If the latter, then all that manager is doing is saying that they are afraid, and they want everything, and everyone, to constantly speed up in response to that fear. In other words, such managers are not managing anything. They are simply running away from something. This is not management, it is panic.

When a manager constantly tells people to go faster but does not know or name a specific mutually agreeable speed, the employees will have to pick the speed for them. When this happens, the manager has, in effect, given up all authority. The people who are endlessly told to "hurry up" decide how fast they are going to work, not the manager. Such managers often curse the "mental slowness" or "stupidity" of their employees, not realizing that they themselves are being "back-managed" by a Principle of Applied Stupidity.

The whole concept of desiring "faster thinking in the workplace" is an obsolete artefact from the days of the industrial revolution. There is a common tendency to take old strategies and try to make them fit new situations. We have inherited a massive legacy of factory management philosophy, and the presumption that "faster speed and greater efficiency are always good" is a big part of that. We all have some nostalgia for the simple days of the past, but the minds of your workers (and the minds of your customers) are not steam-driven looms. Try as you might to make them so, human minds are not machines.

In the realm of generic commodities, sure, faster and cheaper is always good. However, there are no prizes for playing *Beethoven's Fifth* faster than another orchestra. In the modern "thought worker" economy, faster is not necessarily better.

Incompetence as a Management Tool

There is an old saying in business that many companies succeed, not because of their management, but in spite of it. People say this and laugh like it means nothing, but . . . wait a second.

While collective wisdom always condemns incompetent management, this common attitude does not appreciate the enormous power of stupidity, and the managerial advantages that can be achieved through incompetence and disorganization.

I once had the privilege of working with an incredibly incompetent manager. At least, we all thought he was incompetent–but he kept his job because somehow, at the 11th hour, essential tasks were always completed by his team.

One of the primary ways we felt this manager was so incompetent was that he was always springing stuff on us at the last minute, with deadlines of major projects only 48 hours away. I was a consultant, not a staff employee, so one day, after observing this behavior on his part, and yet again suffering through a panicked 48 hour work-athon to get something done all at the last minute, I asked him why he did this repeatedly.

With remarkable candor, he explained his methodology to me. He started by telling that people only do what is urgent. That meant that if he told his staff that something had to be completed six months from now, he knew they would not get focused on it until it was almost too late, and then they will be distracted by the attendant shame on their part for not having done it before the last minute. So if he waited, and told them about it the same time they would have started on it anyway, his staff could blame him for all the stress, instead of themselves. That kept the staff from getting into a personal shame spiral, and they could do their work more effectively. Also, when his staff was able to achieve the goals 'in spite of' his apparent incompetence, it was a great morale booster and confidence builder. They took even more satisfaction from the work itself, which was otherwise somewhat repetitive. They were able to believe that they were that much smarter than both himself and their peers in general.

He also shared this little gem: *Parkinson's Law* states that all tasks will expand to fill the time allotted to them. That means that if he were to give his staff six months to do a job, it would take them six months to do it. By only giving them 48 hours to do it, that gave him five months and 28 days of staff time to use for other tasks.

He concluded by telling me that when time becomes terribly pressing, people who are normally highly obedient to past procedures and protocols will momentarily have the courage to abandon those standard procedures, and they will think and act much more creatively. If they were not rushed, and instead were given excessive amounts of time, they would use that time to maintain the old process. They would shoehorn the current task into the old process, instead of using their imaginations to create a new and better process to efficiently handle the current job.

There you have it.

In sum, while most people condemn incompetent management as being "stupid," there is something to be said for the creative inspiration one derives from a state of total panic and confusion. At such times, you will often discover that you have capabilities that, in slow times of quiet calm and reflection, you never imagined you possessed. It's hard on the body, but one can argue that purely from a short-term immediate productivity standpoint, in certain situations, crazed/stupid/incompetent management can actually work just as well as, or even better than, calm/intelligent/competent management. This leads us to:

Principle #16:
Imminent Disaster, Whether Real, Contrived,
or Just Perceived, Is a Universal Motivator.

Now that you are aware of this principle, along with having the option of using it on others, you may also have occasion to deal with someone else using it on you. Again, stupidity to the rescue.

The reason this principle works so well is that so many people fall into a trap of smartism. It is very easy to believe the delicious idea that the distressed manager became distressed due to their relatively lower intelligence. Rescuing them is, of course, annoying, but also carries with it the imaginary but blissful state of thinking you are demonstrating your superior intellect. Your intelligence, if not put in check, will make you an endless victim.

To counter the effects of the above listed Principle #16, you must be able to respond with several Principles of Applied Stupidity all at once. These include: 1) embracing your inner idiot 2) not automatically solving the problem,* and 3) calmly accepting the possibility of failure.* You can politely express a desire to help, but by taking the high ground of greater stupidity, you will regain control of the situation. The problem remains *their* problem, and your day suddenly becomes calm and orderly again.

* *See future chapters for discussion of the benefits of not solving problems and accepting failure.*

*　　*　　*

While the above-mentioned manager used principle #16 as a subterfuge, you can also use this principle openly and honestly. To illustrate, instead of imminent disaster, let's use a word usually frowned upon, i.e., "risk."

The concept of "risk" is generally thought of as a bad thing, but the fact is, risk creates excitement. There are many people who, because modern life has become so devoid of risk, will go out and deliberately choose to engage in risky behavior, such as mountain climbing. Why would anyone choose such a risk? Simple. It's exciting.

I used to work in live television, and the pressure was horrendous. Why didn't I go and get a nice stress-free job? I'll tell you why: because I enjoyed the excitement. There was always a clear difference in the overall energy of the team when we were "live" as opposed to "taped." We knew that if we made a mistake in a taping session, we could (yawn) just go back and do it over, where the live shows made everyone work at their highest levels of intensity. It was a rush. It was a thrill. Offering people a chance to do something "risky" can be a great motivator. If you do it right, accepting higher risks of possible negative consequences can draw out higher positive energy in response . . . much greater than what you would get if there is no risk involved.

Some people say it's stupid to take risks. Well, to each their own. If you always avoid risk, good for you, but in doing so you risk living a very boring life.

"I changed the conditions of the test. I got a commendation for original thinking. I don't like to lose."
> *–Captain James T. Kirk, commenting on how he was the only person ever to win in the "Kobayashi Maru" no-win scenario*

Stupidity and Proper Procedure

One of the main definitions of "smart" is doing things "right," while one of the main definitions of "stupid" is doing things "wrong." Again, like so many expressions of personal disapproval, the accusation of "wrongness" can be very powerful, so much so that it can stop you from taking a risk on new and untried–but possibly better–ideas. However, you can respond to this problem very effectively, simply by embracing stupidity. By not engaging in a knee-jerk avoidance of stupidity/wrongness labeling, a much larger range of options will open up to you.

To see how this works in real life, let's suppose you want to get a job doing something really fun, like being a rock star. To do this the "right" way, there are schools where you can go to take lessons and classes. You could easily get a bachelor's degree, or even get a master's degree and a Ph.D., in rock and roll-ology. There are lots of people who will create a syllabus for you and, after you have paid your tuition, they will sign papers saying you have all the necessary qualifications to do the job. It all sounds great of course, but no matter how well you do on your final exams, there is absolutely no guarantee that you will ever get a single gig, or even have a chance to perform anywhere.

Conversely, if you have no schooling at all, it is still quite possible to go to the top of the charts. Some of the most famous musicians in the world never went to music school. Some of them can't even read music. Clearly, this is the "wrong" way to go about it, and yet, very often, it still seems to work.

Steven Spielberg is a marvelous example of not following correct procedure. He was not accepted to film school, due to his C grade average in high school. His "procedure" for getting into the movie business involved sneaking off a tour bus at Universal Studios and setting up a phony office for himself in a movie production building. After a while, everyone on staff just assumed that he worked there. Four years later, when his peer group was graduating from film school, he was already directing broadcast television shows. This was hardly a proper or correct procedure, but it worked.

The point of all this is, correct "procedure" is not a reliable system for getting a really plum job. Most people who have plum jobs will tell you a bizarre tale of how they got their job. Such stories rarely involve going through some lengthy, proper, available-to-anyone-and-everyone procedure. Instead, the story usually involves a series of unlikely serendipitous events that ran blatantly *counter* to "proper procedure."

While there is of course no one simple "trick" to getting a plum job, there are a number of ways that the Principles of Applied Stupidity can be an enormous help.

First of all, it is important to get past one of the most cherished tenets of smartist culture, which is that, if you conform to and follow "procedure," you will succeed. Yes, if you follow procedure, you can probably succeed at getting a job frying hamburgers–but getting a position that is a little more profitable and unusual, well, not so true. Many hundreds of thousands of people seek careers in music performance or art history. They carefully follow all the rules and procedures, the get all the degrees and certifications, and yet they still fail to get a job in those fields.

When the failure comes, most of these people assume that they failed because they did not follow the procedures carefully enough, when in fact the opposite is usually the case. Procedures proudly offer themselves as safe gateways to success, but most of the time, following procedure actually leads to failure.

This is because, for highly sought-after positions, we use

Principle #17:
Procedures Are Not Designed to Find People, They Are Designed to Get Rid of Them.

There are four very important things to know about procedures:

1) Procedures immediately put you in a situation where you are surrounded by your strongest competitors;

2) Following procedures makes it difficult for anyone to see any difference between you and your competitors;

3) Even though procedures always claim to exist for your benefit, procedures are ALWAYS designed to benefit the person who designed the procedure, not you, and

4) There is usually someone on the other side of a procedure—i.e., a person who is looking for one person out of a thousand applicants—who wants to avoid going through all of the many dull steps of the procedure if they can.

When talking about seeking a plum job, following procedure is not only not very helpful, it can actually be counter to the success you seek. Therefore it is best make yourself as unaware

78

of "proper procedure" as possible.

If you follow procedure in a highly competitive environment, statistics are not on your side. The most likely thing to happen is that you will be rejected, as the whole point of procedure is to winnow people out. The person who is supervising the procedure is usually eager to get the whole thing over with, and will reject you on the slightest pretext.

However, if you ignore procedure, right off the bat you have made yourself stand out from the crowd. Yes, you are doing something "stupid," as you are demonstrating a total lack of knowledge of how things are supposed to be done. However, in doing so you have drawn special attention to yourself, possibly from a person with real power and not just a lower level bureaucratic gatekeeper. This gives you a very good shot at beating the entire pack, as you are giving the person in charge a quick, simple, and easy solution to their problem. A live person who has barged in will always be victorious over a stack of 300 polite resumes. In fact, the more of these process-following competitors you have, the easier it is to beat them, as they make themselves cumulatively unappealing by their sheer volume and similarity.

At the very least, if you must follow proper procedure, be the very last person to send in the form. That will put you on the top of the pile.

Stupidity and Standards

Many years ago, when I was a professional musician, I of course belonged to the union. Every year, a little booklet was sent out by the union to all of its members. This highly informative little tome listed all the many union pay scales for just about every kind of musical job you could name. These included the various "minimum scales" for playing operas, ballets, television commercials, movie soundtracks, bar mitzvahs, and so on.

I am very grateful for what union membership did for me at the time, as I certainly had no skills at negotiating fees or contracts. These "minimum scales" were very appealing, as they offered a quick boost to my economic situation.

However, after a few years of working at all these union jobs for minimum scale, an interesting fact came to light: While I never got paid any less than minimum scale, I never got paid any *more* than minimum scale either. This is a perfect of illustration of

Principle #18:
The Minimum Is the Maximum.

Here is another illustration of this principle at work: let's suppose you go into the Department of Motor Vehicles, and they tell you that the *minimum* fee for your license renewal is $40. Of course, you want your license to be renewed, so you meet this minimum requirement. Now honestly, are you going to pay any *more* than $40? Did such an idea even enter your mind? Of course not. You certainly aren't going to give them any more than you absolutely have to. This is exactly what happens so often with minimum standards. They become the maximum standard as well.

"Minimum standards" are one of the most prevalent symptoms of smartist thinking. Minimum standards always look good on paper, because when they are compared to the benchmark of no one doing much of anything (which is usually the result of everyone meeting the previous set of minimum standards), the imposition of a new set of minimum standards promises, or at least gives hope for, an immediate and obvious bit of desperately needed improvement. Unfortunately, what so often gets overlooked in the revolving door concept of minimum standards is that they become the maximum standard as well.

You must always be careful when someone starts talking about imposing minimum standards, because whether you are talking about a school or a workplace, if you impose a minimum standard, you are also imposing a maximum standard. When people are given a minimum standard to meet, well, like your day at the DMV, the majority of people will meet the minimum standard and go no further.

Minimum standards, as the phrase implies, are usually pretty low, since they have to be "meet-able" by just about everyone, or at least large numbers of unmotivated people. And of course, they appear to be even lower when compared to infinite potential.

Some people are so used to having minimum standards imposed on them that they have no concept of doing things any other way. The idea of a "no-standards" environment is totally foreign to them.

In case you have never heard of a "no-standards" environment, well, one of the best examples is a major symphony orchestra. You may find it odd to hear me say that "the Boston Symphony Orchestra has no standards," but this is precisely the case. Since there are no minimum standards, there is no implied finish line. There is no point at which one can be satisfied and go home. Instead, lacking any minimum standard, the standard becomes whatever is the absolute best you can do today (and hopefully better tomorrow), and so on into infinity. The standard, if you can even call it that, is unattainable. Since it doesn't exist, it can never met, it can only be striven for. Also, since that culture has no minimum standards to spread you thin all over the place in multiple areas, you are free to put every ounce of available energy into the single note you are playing right now. This kind of total focus is key to world-class performance. The existence of minimum standards tends to dilute energy into a number of places, instead of letting you focus all your energy in one place in order to achieve the highest possible "maximum" performance.

Sadly, you often see this Principle at work in many work and school environments. There is often much talk of "minimum standards," with very good intentions and lots of self-congratulation by those who are making and implementing these standards, but like union pay scales, or the amount of money you have to pay for renewing your car registration, or the requirement of every single kid to know the exact same smattering of biology, chemistry, and history whether they are interested or not, those minimum standards, once met, with few exceptions, become maximum standards. Once people meet the minimum standard needed to get what they want from you, they stop. Once the test is crammed for and passed, everything stops right there, as all further interest and motivation is nonexistent. In effect, the imposition of a minimum standard generally becomes a maximum standard. Such standards are, at best, a tolerance (or even a design) for mediocrity, and, at their worst, an insidious form of social, intellectual, and economic repression.

The minimum . . . is the maximum.

"I remind people that, like when I'm with Condoleeza Rice, I say she's the Ph.D. and I'm the C student, and just look at who's the president and who's the advisor."
                                        –George W. Bush

Stupidity and Politics

When it comes to presidential politics, most of us find ourselves locked in the throes of smartism.

On the one hand, we tell our friends that we think we should all go out and get the smartest and brightest person that we possibly find to be the president. On the other hand, in our heart of hearts, we really don't want a president who thinks he (or she) is smarter than the rest of us.

This is because we really believe that if the president thinks he (or she) is smarter than we are, they will go off on their own and do what they think is good for us instead of listening to us. If you recall Principle #12 (Information Flows from Smart to Dumb), this means smart people generally don't listen to dumb people. Given that tendency, it is reasonable to assume that if the president is smarter than us, it is doubtful that such a president will ever listen to our concerns.

While the average CEO can afford to be seen ignoring the common workers, in politics, this is death. No matter how smart you may be, if people think you are aren't listening to them, they will not vote for you, so . . . if you are a presidential candidate, it's generally good to downplay your intellectual capacity. You should tell voters that you think *they* are much smarter than *you*. What may sound like self-denigration actually translates into

83

people thinking you respect them, and so you will therefore listen to them. This is a very important application of the Principles of Applied Stupidity.

The Irregardless Effect

Mistakes are your friend.

This statement probably sounds odd to you. After all, you spent many years in school, and you were constantly told to not make mistakes. Worse, in that stress-filled culture, you were probably laughed at or publicly embarrassed if you were caught making any mistakes.

The emotional trauma you experienced was supposedly justified, because training you to not make errors was, in that system anyway, more important than anything else, including your spiritual and emotional well-being. It is time to enter a different dimension.

As previously mentioned, the universal obsession with perfection (or at least the avoidance of errors) as taught by smartist culture is extremely limiting. Far from being a sin to be always avoided, mistakes can be used for all sorts of marvelous purposes.

Just to give you one example:

There was this guy who owned a car dealership.

This guy had an unusual technique for business development. Every time a new customer came in and bought a new car, this guy would wait about two weeks after the car was delivered, and then he would send this new customer a little note. The note would say, "We're so sorry, we made an error on your final invoice. We accidentally overcharged you $27.49. Please accept our apologies. Your refund check is enclosed."

Now hang on a minute. Mistakes are supposed to be BAD, right? And admitting to a mistake is even worse, right? So why pretend to make a mistake? And worse, why admit to it?

Well . . . every single customer who received this unexpected rebate became convinced that this guy was the first (and only) honest car salesman they had ever met. They instantly became loyal customers forever. Of course, he made back the measly $27.49 on the first service visit, not to mention how much money he made when he sold them (and all of their friends) their next car.

There are many other wonderful uses of intentional mistake-making. Just to give you another example:

Fighter pilots often use the phrase "target fascination." This term refers to becoming so focused on the enemy plane in front of you– i.e., the one you hope to shoot down–that you lose track of the enemy plane that is lining up behind you, which, incidentally, is hoping to shoot *you* down.

Something very similar happens with mistakes.

When people encounter a large mistake or error of some sort, they suffer from "error fascination." All they can see is the one big mistake; everything else becomes invisible to them. There can be other mistakes, or all kinds of other stuff going on, but after years and years of relentless smartist training in "mistakes are evil," their senses and perceptions are overwhelmed by the one large error. It's like someone shining a bright light in your eyes in a dimly lit room. Your iris closes down, and all you can see is the bright light and nothing else.

This oh-so-common phenomenon makes it very easy to manipulate many situations, simply by using what is known as the "Irregardless Effect." The Irregardless Effect is expressed in

Principle #19:
People Are So Fascinated by Large Mistakes That They Will Fail to Notice Little Mistakes, or Anything Else for That Matter.

The Irregardless Effect is achieved by making a blatant and very obvious error, one that everyone in the room will immediately and collectively recognize as such. When a large error is presented, everyone in the room will become totally mesmerized by the error, and they will not see, or be able to think about, anything else.

The reason mistakes are so mesmerizing is because mistakes remind most people of the emotional trauma that was visited upon them in grade school. Even though they have not made the mistake themselves, the presence of a mistake will typically make them freeze up in a flashback of unbearable blocked-out memories.

Given how we have been trained to associate mistake-making with severe emotional trauma, it will no doubt seem rather odd that you, or anyone else, would purposefully make an obvious error in full view of everyone. That is why the Irregardless Effect works so well. Since most people are governed by Principle #5 (Fear of Looking Stupid Is an Enormous Force), they will also assume that everyone else is also terribly afraid of looking stupid, therefore it will never occur to them that you or anyone else would actually make a mistake on purpose. As a result, when you display a huge contrived error, this fascinates the average observer. They are now under the spell of the Irregardless Effect.

They will be so fascinated by that one big contrived mistake you have put in front of them that they will not notice anything else you may be doing. Once the Irregardless Effect is in play, you can pretty much get away with anything, and you can do so right under their noses.

Just to give you one quick example: there was once a video producer who often utilized the Irregardless Effect in his line of work (in fact, he used it on me for years, and this is how I learned the technique).

This fellow was in the business of creating little "industrial" videos for corporate clients (to show at company meetings, etc). When he made preliminary versions of these little TV shows, he knew he would have to deal with a lot of middle managers who had authority to critique the production. Most of them, of course, knew virtually nothing about video or movie production, but they all wanted to help. "Rub their smell on the project" is the phrase he used.

Anyway, when he created "final approval" versions of the show to present to these middle managers, he would put a really obvious error in the show. This would be something like a misspelled name of the company's CEO, or worse, sometimes he would even misspell the name of the company itself.

When the various vice-presidents would come in to view one of these "final approval" versions, of course, they would all immediately see this planted error. Right on cue, they would all jump up in a fit of smartist ecstacy and say, "Oh my goodness, you made such a terrible mistake, good thing I was here to catch it."

This producer would then proceed to act very obsequiously, pretending to be very dumb and saying "Oh my gosh, I'm so glad you were here to catch that awful mistake."

With their need to feel smart having been satisfied, all the people in fancy suits would then walk out of the meeting feeling important and vindicated, and no major difficult changes had to be made. (In fact, the show with the correct spelling was usually already done, just in case no one caught the blatant error). The correction of the phony error would be the sum total of the clients' input, as the one huge error so effectively overwhelmed their perceptions that everything else looked great to them in comparison. It was a very simple, yet very effective, application of the Irregardless Effect and the Principles of Applied Stupidity.

By the way, please don't be too quick to condemn this guy. There was a very good reason why he planted these intentional "stupid mistakes." As you know, people in middle management positions generally feel compelled to justify their high salaries. If there was no obvious error to find, they would still feel obligated to find *something* to change . . . maybe something that shouldn't be changed. By planting a faux error to find, he cut down on amateurish meddling, while making clients "take ownership" of the project by making them think they had made a major contribution.

Next, here is another example of masterful use of the Irregardless Effect, used by none other than George W. Bush. This was done in full view of millions of people, but, due to the power of the Irregardless Effect, no one noticed it:

Sandra Day O'Connor, the first woman to ever serve on the Supreme Court, retired a few years ago, and it was up to George W. to appoint her successor. Now there is nothing in the Constitution about how many women need to be on the supreme court, but it was pretty much assumed that to be politically correct, etc., another woman should be nominated to replace O'Connor. So George nominated . . . Harriet Miers. I have never met the woman, and I am sure she is very nice, but she had never served as a judge. An interesting choice.

When this nomination was announced, a lot of people, both

Republican and Democrat, and even the ones who wanted a woman to be appointed, jumped up and said, "Good grief, this woman is totally unqualified." There was a big political hooha, and the nomination was rejected. So Bush's next nominee—who just happened to be a man—had credentials that looked so good relative to Ms. Miers that he sailed through the confirmation process.

George W. killed two birds with one rock here. While he appeared to be doing something that everyone thought was incredibly stupid, he got free of an implied requirement to nominate a woman. ("I nominated a woman and they turned her down." What a great excuse.) He also got tremendous leeway in who he could pick, as anyone he nominated with even an ounce of actual judging experience was going to look like a star in comparison.

The Irregardless Effect is so powerful that it can be used with great effect on people in positions of authority above you, but of course it can also be used to manage subordinates as well.

For example, let's suppose you have five assistants. You want their input on a PowerPoint Project or a memorandum, or perhaps you just want them to proofread a letter. You want to make sure that they are actually reading it and not just avoiding work by telling you it's fine as is. How do you do this? It's very simple: you just put in some obvious errors.

You can certainly use your own imagination, but to start you off, you can use things like "its" where it should be "it's." Phrases like "they was" are always good, and of course there's the gold standard of bad writing, which of course is the word "irregardless." If you sprinkle any or all of these errors into a document draft, and someone that you have assigned to edit and/or critique the work says it's fine as is, you know you have a shirker on your hands.

Most bosses would cringe at the thought of being caught making a mistake that was viewable by an underling, but it's a fabulous way to test for due diligence. Because of Principle #6 (Everyone Wants to Look and Feel Smart), people love to comment on mistakes you have made, and if someone doesn't comment on a mistake you have made, there is a 99% chance that this is not because they are being polite, it's because they did not do their homework.

Of course, there is a small drawback to this problem, which is, once they see the word "irregardless" and fix it, the rest of your document will look fabulous in comparison, warts and all.

This is a very powerful Principle of Applied Stupidity. You should use it with caution, and at your own risk.

Enhancing Creativity with Stupidity

One of the most effective uses of Applied Stupidity is in the realm of creativity.

The creative abilities of different people often get ranked and compared, but you should not buy into the idea that creativity can be treated as a generic commodity, any more than you should accept the universal rankings of intelligence. When you look at even the most average children at play, you see their imaginations working at a fever pitch. You will rarely see one five-year-old kid, in a kindergarten finger-painting session, say to another kid, "gosh, you're so creative." There are many different kinds of creative ability, and everyone is creative.

We tend to think that childlike creativity and imagination are lost at the onset of puberty, but this does not have to happen to you. If you would like to rediscover your creative ability, one excellent way to do it is to employ the Principles of Applied Stupidity; in this case, we use

Principle #20:
Stupidity Is a Breeding Ground for
New Ideas and Innovation in General.

Let's begin by asking this question: how does your creativity work? Well, here is one version: It starts with your mind somehow receiving an idea. (This might come from the deep recesses of your mind, or maybe, as Buckminster Fuller used to hypothesize, it might come as a ray of inspiration from the cosmos.) When that little seed of an idea presents itself, you are essentially the mother of a fragile figurative embryo. Your mind is its womb, and for a while that new idea is totally dependent upon you for sustaining its life. Children take great joy in this feeling. Having these fantastic images and/or new ideas pop into their heads is so exciting and feels so good that they offer no resistance to this process. Unfortunately, as time goes on, as in so many areas of life, the need to avoid looking stupid and the desire to look smart ruin all the fun.

It's easy to understand why we would repress expression of our creativity as soon as we are old enough to do so. Our imaginations are wild and unpredictable. We often come up with stuff that, at first glance, is nonsensical and therefore "stupid," i.e., embarrassing. Also, since our imaginings are a direct extension of our souls, the open expression of these imperfect ideas makes us feel vulnerable and exposed (another common definition of "feeling stupid"). As we grow up, we find that our raw outbursts of creativity generally fail to conform to narrow definitions of correct "intelligent" behavior; thus, they are labeled as "stupid."

To avoid feeling/looking/being called stupid, we quickly learn to keep our own unique ideas hidden away and express only those ideas that we know are safely "pre-approved." We train ourselves to avoid letting anyone else see any spontaneous expressions of our imaginations. The trouble is, after years and years of keeping them hidden from others, one day we discover that there is an unexpected and unpleasant side effect, which is, now we can't see them ourselves either. We often don't notice this until one day, when we have a chance to "do something creative," we hit a blank wall, as our imaginations are calloused over from years of neglect and habitual repression.

The real answer to the challenge of rediscovering lost creativity is not to try to re-learn how to do it. You already know how to do it. That skill and capacity has always been there. The trick is to override the anti-stupid protectionist machinery that is blocking your view of it.

To re-acquire full access to your creativity, start with Principle #10 (that is, accepting your inner idiot). This is essential to the creative process, as it does two things: 1) it lessens the repression of new ideas for fear of their being condemned by others, i.e., being thought stupid, and 2) it frees up resources that are currently being devoted to "looking smart" by demonstrating knowledge of old ideas.

Once you embrace your inner idiot, then you don't have to *worry* about looking like an idiot. This will eliminate wasted brain cycles and enhance your creative output considerably. Remember, Stupidity Science is all about doing less. In this case, stop expending your brainpower on worrying about potential bad consequences, or what other people will think of your ideas, or why they may not work. Once you do that, you can get back to happily processing the constant output of your imagination.

Again, the trick is to accept your so-called stupidity. Once you do that, the worst that can happen has already happened. Once you do that, even if people think you are an idiot, you have already accepted that worst case yourself, so you have nothing to lose. You are now free to let your imagination run wild.

The other reason you need to use Principle #10 is that, in response to your own fear of looking stupid, you have very likely become very critical of your own ideas, perhaps more so than anyone else. By applying stupidity, you will gleefully lower your standards for the first draft of your new ideas. This is very important, because almost every new idea is flawed at the start, therefore every new idea can be defined by you or someone else as being "stupid."

Despite what you may have been taught, creativity is not about having *West Side Story* fall out of your head in a couple of hours. Yes, Mozart could do amazing stuff on the first pass, but for most people, ideas in their nascent form are generally "stupid" in the sense that they are unworkable. They have flaws. They are confusing and contradictory, and they usually don't address the seemingly impossible logistical problems of executing them. (The list of resistance to new ideas in endless. For example,"if these new ideas were any good, we assume someone else would have thought of it already." And we are especially resistant to ideas when they are in conflict with established ideas, even if the old idea is totally incorrect.)

Once you have removed that clog in the pipe caused by the constant criticism of every little flaw, you will find that you have lots of ideas floating around, some good, some lousy, but in any case, probably more than you can use.

Then the next step: Ideas, like gold, need to be refined. If you go spelunking for a good idea, you will find it mixed in with a lot of lousy ideas. You can't expect any precious mineral to come out of the ground without also finding a lot of useless stuff all around it. Imagination is the ore, and creativity is the ability to appreciate what is buried in the dirt and crud. It is also the willingness to go through the refining process without being constrained by being afraid of people thinking you are doing something dumb before you are finished.

Along with the dampening effect created by always trying to avoid looking stupid, the other great enemy of creativity is too much intelligence.

When trying and failing to be creative, the thing that defeats so many people is that they are too intelligent, i.e., they are too aware of all the other creative work that has already been done. They pass over any idea they have that doesn't immediately compare favorably with Michelangelo's *David*. Their intelligence, knowledge, and training actually become an impediment to their creativity.

Since their own original ideas can't compete with what they have studied, they toss out everything their imaginations share with them. They actually start to inflate their sense of how smart they are, not by measuring their creative output, but by focusing on how ultra-critical they are, and how quickly they can find flaws with every idea they have. One can call this "smart," but of course there is no creativity. They lose faith in their own imaginations and instead become dealers in second-hand ideas.

There is something to be said for being extremely well versed on past events; but if you are constantly stuffing your brain full of existing second-hand information and ideas, and demanding that every new idea must immediately exceed arbitrary performance benchmarks on its first day, you make it that much harder for your own new ideas to find a home. If all the storage capacity of your mind is chock full of stuff, where is there room for new stuff? If your mind gets too packed full of information, like a garden choked with weeds, it's not likely that anything else will take root and grow there. There is just too much competition for available resources. If, on the other hand, you have an empty patch of mental dirt, as any gardener will tell you, even if you try to keep it clear, every day something will start to grow in it.

Every farmer starts the season by plowing under last year's crop. Keeping your mental goober patch clear of the old growth of established thinking and old ideas takes some work. Or perhaps one should say, not work, but restraint. This lack of mental activity is necessary to the creative process. Like any patch of dirt in the temperate zone, creativity happens all by itself unless there is a mulch of old ideas (or an herbicide of ultra criticism) spread all over it. What at first looks like another weed just might be the first page of the next Harry Potter series.

The book you are reading right now started as a single, tiny, almost invisible idea. All there was at the start was the phrase "I got to play with the Boston Pops because I was too dumb to know it was impossible." That was it. There were no outlines, no chapters, no table of contents, no cover design, no ISBN number. At the beginning, I had to work hard to overcome my own resistance to the idea. While there are jillions of books and studies about intelligence, I couldn't find very much information on the subject of stupidity, and I found myself asking, "If it's such a good idea, why hasn't someone else done it already? And after all, a book about stupidity, what could be stupider than THAT?"

But . . . I decided to not let my intelligence judge it too soon. I kept it under wraps, and it just grew from there, a thousand words one day, ten words the next. Even as I write this chapter, only half of the book is written. If I think too much about it how it is so terribly unfinished compared to the millions of books currently in print, I will give up. So I don't think about that. If I think about how I am exposing myself to possible derision from people who will disagree with me, I will give up. So I don't think about that either. Stupidity and mental emptiness are key to the process. By keeping boxes of junk out of the guestroom of my mind, ideas pop into my head when I'm in the shower. I jot them down with no expectation of them being any good. I just let them grow, and I tactfully prune as I go along.

To rediscover your creative spirit, you don't need to find some special access to a mystical fountainhead somewhere. Just don't resist your own ideas. The creativity happens all by itself. Keep the ground clear and watered, and don't weed out every unknown plant right away. You never know what will pop up. The hardest part of being creative is resisting the smartist urge to imitate the old and repress the new.

To enhance your creative output with the use of Applied Stupidity, simply accept yourself as being in a state of not knowing the answer. Yes, not knowing the answer is scary and is potentially a state of "dumbness," but this does not have to be a problem, as this can be readily addressed by the application of Principle #10. There is nothing wrong with being in that state. Send your question out to the cosmos or in to the depths of your brain (the process is identical) and then let your jaw go slack and stupidly wait for the answer. When you wake up tomorrow, it might just pop into your head. Happens to me all the time. You're holding one of those ideas in your hand right now. The difference is not in having the ideas. Everyone has ideas. The difference is in not resisting them. In other words, the difference is the application of stupidity.

Stupidity and Road Runners

Chuck Jones, the director of many Bugs Bunny cartoons, once explained the first step his team took in creating so many classics of animation.

All of the people involved in the design and production of the cartoon would sit down in a room. The writer would stand up and give a brief synopsis of a basic story idea. After that, the team employed a most unusual technique for developing the many creative elements of the cartoon. They called it the "yes session."

There was no real structure to a "yes session" after the presentation of that first script outline. Each person just offered possible ideas for dialogue, sound effects, story, backgrounds, characters, music, whatever. "Yes sessions" had just one very simple rule: no one could say "no." No one was allowed to be negative in any way, or disapprove of any idea that was put forth. Every idea was guaranteed to get approval and acceptance on its first pass, no matter how silly or impractical.

These people understood just how potentially destructive preconceived standards and methods could be to the creative process. They overcame this problem (i.e., Principle #5, Fear of Looking Stupid Is an Enormous Force) with this simple workaround. The absence of structure and standards meant there was no basis for disapproval of anything. This led to far greater creative energy. They accepted the possibility of making mistakes, they constantly encouraged everyone to wander into unknown territory, and they made magic.

Stupidity and Anxiety

Anyone who thinks that people lose the childlike ability of imagination and creativity as they grow up has forgotten about the adult version, which is generally referred to as worrying.

Smartist culture places insidious pressure on you to know everything that needs to be known. If something is not known, then we demand that you be able to figure it out anyway, through scientific means or mathematical equations. Of course, in reality, many things cannot be predicted. Even so, the ever-present need to be smart, or at least avoid looking dumb, leads us to want to know things that cannot be known in advance. When the desire to be "smart" creates an expectation that we must know the answers to questions in advance when no information is available, all too often the imagination steps in to fill the gap.

When we try to predict the future with virtually no facts to go on, our minds—that is, our imaginations—demonstrate their extraordinary creative power of fanciful vision, and they do so in a way that makes schoolchildren at play seem terribly unimaginative by comparison. We can envision an infinite number of bad results, some of which completely defy laws of probability, statistics, and physics; and yet our minds create them in full color and amazingly fine detail. We invest full belief in them, and react physically to these thoughts as if they are actually happening to us.

Worry is a kind of creativity that yes, *is* stupid (in the sense that it deserves blanket disapproval) and yes, should be repressed. However, the way to do this is not to use the methods taught by smartist culture. Smartist culture always teaches you to use more and more brain activity to deal with any situation, even if the problem is too much brain activity. Instead of trying to stop Möbius Strips of thought from circling around in your head by adding more and more thought to the firestorm, you can easily and effectively counter this problem with—you guessed it—Applied Stupidity.

The lack of brain activity can be wonderfully useful in seeking rest, but for many people a restful lack of brain activity is generally associated with shameful feelings of stupidity. As a result, you may sometimes keep your mind working long after you should, instead of resting your brain muscles. Using "meditation" to end useless circular stress-inducing thought is okay, but god forbid you should call this willful studied attempt at calming your mind an attempt to induce stupidity, even though that's exactly what it is.

Principle #21:
Stupidity Is Better than Anxiety.

Stupidity and anxiety both consist of the same substance, i.e., nothing, but only one of them lets you rest and relax and be ready for the moment when you do get some information and can finally act.

It is amazing just how much of the supposed "cleverness" used in worry, i.e., imagining infinite potential negative consequences, is pure wasted effort. Training yourself *not to think* is counter to all smartist training, but doing so saves you from spending precious emotional energy on things you cannot control, so you can devote that energy to more effective happiness-producing activities that you *can* control.

Stupidity and Magic

There is a fellow out in the Midwest somewhere who claims that he can control the weather. Perhaps the word is not "control." Influence might be a better word.

Before we continue, please take a moment to ponder how you reacted to the above statement. Here is some time for you to do this:

.

.

.

.

Okay, that's enough.

What's really interesting about this claim of his is not the claim itself, interesting though it may be. What's really interesting is how people react to it. Consistently, without exception, everyone who hears of this claim immediately refutes it, with only slight variations in their rather high degrees of vehemence. This is puzzling. If someone knows for a fact that controlling the weather is impossible, why do they react with such extreme emotion? Their reaction is best described as similar to being charged 30 dollars for a cup of coffee. They are not just astonished, they are also outraged. Why don't they just react with calm pity for a lost delusional soul?

Someone once asked this fellow, "assuming it is possible that you can do this, how did you figure out how?" In response, he proceeded to tell a story about a cousin of his who had consistently good weather wherever he went. If this relative's lawn needed watering, it rained. If they went to the beach, it was sunny and warm, even in December. If his kid forgot to do his homework, it snowed really hard, enough to cancel school for a day.

He proceeded to say how he observed and pondered these repeated coincidences and phenomena, and said, "I finally figured out how my cousin was able to do it. It was because he was too dumb to know that it was impossible. He just walked around expecting good weather, and it always happened for him."

He then proceeded to explain that he took this example, i.e., of the lack of awareness of the "fact" that we live in a world where no one can control the weather, and just started to experiment with it. He removed the "knowledge" of it being impossible from his head, and now he says it just happens all by itself. He didn't acquire a special power; he says he just removed the belief that it couldn't be done.

The purpose of this book is not to get into a debate as to whether or not such things are possible or impossible. Yes, this could just be a series of odd coincidences, and it probably is. On the other hand, who's to say that it's *not* good karma, or even magic? Who knows? And furthermore, who cares? Since it costs nothing to believe it's something more, why not? Kids who believe in magic and Santa Claus, ignorant of the laws of physics though they may be, generally enjoy life more than the kids who don't.

Lab Activities in Stupidity

Along about now, people who scored 1600 on the SAT will ask, "gosh, this sounds great, but how do I 'act stupid'?"

There is a temptation to say "what a stupid question," but instead of keeping you in intellectual shackles by shaming your honest curiosity, here are a few tips and tricks:

The power of smartist manipulation is derived from your own ego. As long as you feel a need to somehow either please people or prove you are superior (read: minimally socially acceptable) by doing difficult tasks perfectly, you will forever be hosed by people who do not have this problem.

So, when people ask you to do things, if you can't directly say no, then try these alternatives: simply do them poorly, or do them so slowly that they eventually learn not to assign you anything important.

Another trick is to always imply that someone else is better at things than you are, preferably the person doing the asking. A sample conversation:

Lisa:
"Wow, we have this big event for the clients tomorrow and the banquet hall is just so plain looking, Gosh, Suzie, you're so good at this sort of thing, could you (give up your Friday night and Saturday morning for no extra pay and) do something up for us?"

Suzie:
(Smart response:) "Well, Lisa, gee whiz, since no one else but me is qualified to do it, and since someone thinks it's not perfect and it needs to be made perfect in order to make the event superior to all other sales events in the known universe, even though this will have no tangible benefit or impact other than impressing *your* boss with *your* work, I guess I can do that."

Now compare the above to the following "Stupid" response:

"Oh, Lisa, that is a great a idea. You are so smart, but I really have no idea how to do that. In any event, I am sure you must be better at that than me. I have an idea: I would love to see you do the decorations so I could learn from you. By the way, I can't stand on ladders without getting a nosebleed and I'm color blind. But you're right, even though I can't quite visualize it, I think it would be great, and I'm with you all the way."

This way, instead of sounding like you are lazy or have an attitude problem, you sound like you care and want to help but are simply unable to do so due to your own genetic shortcomings. This automatically works, because even though you are just dodging extra work, you did it by telling Lisa she is smarter than you are, and Lisa will usually buy into this because of Principle #6 (Everyone Wants to Look and Feel Smart).

Amazingly, once this little ritual is dispensed with, the problem usually gets solved by itself. This is because once people lose hope of getting something done for free, the whole idea usually just goes away, and suddenly the meeting room looks great as is. And if you still get your arm twisted, well, since the work is "so arduous and difficult" for you, you are in a position to charge for your time, and actually get more than they would pay you if you were a smart "qualified person." If you're brilliant, it's a lot harder to justify the invoice, as it was "so easy for you."

Whenever anyone asks a leading question that might lead to more work for no money, don't let your smartist ego lead you into "saving the day." When in doubt, do nothing. Move slowly. Be accepting of failure. This is the beauty of accepting your inner idiot, as everything else just naturally flows from that one simple idea. The moment you make the mistake of looking smart, and you let on that you are emotionally invested in achieving outcomes that are above the bare minimum requirement, people will try to get you to donate that extra effort for free. They will imply that your superior ability obligates you to donate more of your time, as you need to compensate for all the other poor unfortunates in the world who don't have your "gifts" (all of whom, by the way, are sitting on their yachts this weekend).

There is one very common kind of victim of smartist training, and this is what is sometimes referred to as the "office mouse." This person is typically exhausted from doing virtually everything for everyone, usually for very little money.

If you are one of these people, the answer to your problem is very simple: start thinking of yourself as being intellectually inferior, but still deserving in every way, and perhaps more so, since you are "less intelligent." (You will be amazed at how well this works.) Your answer to every question should become either "I don't know," "I don't know how to do that," or "Well I could do it I guess, but it would take like [insert ridiculously long period of time here]."

Unlike second grade, where you were eager to do timed tests perfectly and quickly, do the opposite. Do things inaccurately and slowly. Be accepting of C's and D's. Make it so that, whatever it is that someone is asking you to do, it would take the same amount of time and effort (or maybe less time and effort) for them to simply do it themselves. Never do work that is better than what the person assigning it to you could do. They have no business saying that it is unacceptable, because to do so would say that their own work is also unacceptable as well.

It's also a good idea to make a few hard-to-find errors in every job. This makes for a situation where bosses have to check every bit of any work assigned to you, and very often that is more energy- and time-consuming than simply doing it themselves.

Instead of trying to compensate yourself for your low pay and long hours by telling yourself how intellectually superior you are to your idiot bosses, start emulating your idiot bosses.

And even more important, always tell them how much smarter they are than you. This will cover a multitude of sins. Put stupidity to work for you.

*   *   *

Another area where stupidity can be very effectively applied in the workplace has to do with the issue of promotions.

Many people make the common assumption that the smartest person always gets hired and/or promoted. This just isn't so. There was a guy in one company who used his hiring authority to make sure no one under him in his group was qualified to do his job. That way, there was no easy way for him to be fired or forced into retirement, as everyone else in the company knew that none of his assistants were qualified to replace him. Of course when he finally did retire, that department fell apart for a few years, but that was not his problem.

Nobody wants competition, so if one vice president can give input on who will be promoted up to their same level, well of course, the person who is least intelligent will get their vote, as that unintelligent person will make them look so good by comparison. (Of course, this creates a problem for that smart VP, in that the new hire will of course make them look ever more intelligent, hence more threatening to the next level of people. Sad to say, all too often, that smart VP ends up stuck where they are, and the "stupid" person continues up the ladder. Stupidity is a double edged sword.)

While everyone is so fascinated with looking smart themselves, it is always better to hire someone smarter than you and let them do all the work. The smart people you hire will be threatening enough to others, so you don't have to worry about them being a threat to you.

True, if you are the most intelligent person, that might make you indispensable. Good for you. But it also means that you cannot be replaced, so that means you cannot be promoted. There is always a belief that a stupid-looking person can somehow be trained to fill a higher management position. Also, stupid-looking people always project an aura of massive unfulfilled potential. A smart person is always maxed out and indispensable where they are, so there they stay.

Fools and Their Money

We live in a culture where money is awfully important, and so we must constantly deal with the presence of people who are trying to get our money from us at every turn.

While one should not be totally careless about handling money, there are number of areas where stupidity can help you a lot in financial matters. One is being aware of the power of Principle #6 (Everyone Wants to Look and Feel Smart), and how smartist culture will try to manipulate you by appealing to your need to look smart all the time.

Just as one example, every time you get a promotional e-mail from some electronics store, what is shown in the largest print? Is it the name of the product, what it will do for you, or god forbid how much it will actually cost you? No. The biggest print is reserved for telling you how much you will *save*.

Of course, spending less money is an appealing idea, and in general it sounds good and makes a certain amount of sense; but trying to distill some little piece of smartist self-esteem out of such things is a huge mistake. Many people are vulnerable to this little sugar cube of imagined cleverness, and we will spend 950 dollars in order to say that we "saved" 50. That's our victory, that we got taken for $950 instead of $1000. Hooray.

In order to feel smarter than someone who paid full price (but who got immediate access to the latest technology and probably bought it solely because of its usefulness to them, therefore the price was not a major issue, as they gained much more profit and enjoyment and use out of the item directly), we will buy something that we don't really need. Were it not for the little ego rush of supposedly outsmarting someone else who paid more for it, we would probably never buy it.

It is truly amazing just how often these techniques gets used, and just how deceitful most pricing systems are. One of the most bizarre applications of this technique is in the realm of "list prices." Take the book business: in theory, the "list price" is the price of the book, but in practice no one charges list price except maybe a few independent bookstores. In this little game, publishers decide how much they want to actually make, then they calculate how much they have to inflate that price to a "list price" that no one will ever be asked to pay, to allow for the discounts from list price that will be offered by discount on-line sellers. All this is done to distract and hoodwink people, and create a sense, not of a positive interaction and exchange of real value, but simply of outsmarting someone else by "getting a deal" and "saving" money.

Many other businesses employ these deceptive inflation/ discount games as well. It's probably because they work. It works on me all the time.

So here are some questions one should always ask: How much time gets wasted in your day for the purpose of chasing a smart feeling? Have you ever saved 30% off the list price of an item you did not need? Have you ever waited in line at a grocery store service counter for more than 10 minutes to get a 30 cent refund? Or even worse, have you ever spent three hours filling out microscopic rebate forms from computer stores, in order to save five dollars? An objective cost-benefit analysis consistently shows that such activities are totally idiotic, and yet we continue to seek that ephemeral brief ego surge acquired by "saving" money.

The need to feel smart is a powerful one, and people who do not learn and apply Principle #10 (Embracing Your Inner Idiot) can easily be manipulated with these techniques. Just to start, try counting how often you are told that buying a certain product is the "smart" thing to do, or that the product itself is somehow smart– smart food, smart cars, smart banking, the list goes on and on.

Of course there is a flip side to smartness and trying to save money, and that's the need to "avoid looking stupid" reflex that might stop you from investing in a long shot. No one knows if it's smart or dumb to invest in a risky venture until afterwards. For some people, the risk of an investment is not just about the risk of losing the money. It's also about the risk of "looking stupid" for having lost your money. Real risk-takers understand the importance of Principle #10. Only those who are willing to risk "looking stupid" ever make a killing.

Our modern definitions of smart and dumb are expressions of emotion. Money is also largely an expression of emotion, i.e., an expression of what we want. Our use of these emotional concepts pretends to be based on logical objective criteria, but this is rarely the case. Accepting this, and accepting the power of the words smart and stupid, will make you less susceptible to those who would use these forces against you.

A smart shopper and their money are soon parted.

Stupidity and Problem Solving (Part I)

One of the most common tenets of smartist dogma is the belief that problems and obstacles need to be addressed with intelligence, i.e., by problem solving and brainwork, and no other response or method is considered to even exist. While there is a certain amount of efficacy in this approach, it is not the only approach that can work. Sometimes, when you are faced with a problem, intelligence exacerbates the problem, and worse, sometimes intelligence itself is the problem.

Intelligence can be the problem because of how we are trained to use our intelligence to react to problems.

For example, when you encounter a problem, smartist training teaches that it *must be solved*, as failure to do so is shamed by being called stupid. Also, problems tend to come in bunches, and the general experience of lesson plans and getting promoted from one grade to the next requires that problems *must always be solved in an orderly series*. This means you must always answer question "A" before going on to question "B," and you must take course 101 before going on to course 102, and so on.

The math teacher at my high school was a great believer in this linear approach. He made us keep a notebook of all our homework. Even if you forgot to do your homework, yeah, you got an "F" for the day, but that wasn't the end of it. It wasn't like you could just mourn the loss and get on with your life. No, at the end of the year, the notebook had to have all the homework assignments in it. Even though there was no credit for a late assignment, you still had to go back and do the previous night's homework along with the new homework.

Some might say this sort of linear approach teaches discipline and organization, yada yada yada. Yes, it creates a possible mental advantage of training you to always think in a linear fashion, but it also creates a possible mental *dis*advantage . . . of training you to always think in a linear fashion. Linear thinking is fine, but there are many other ways of thinking, and linear thinking isn't always the best way to achieve your goal.

For example, let's suppose that you are presented with a series of, say, 26 problems, going from A to Z.

However, let's also say that you are only really interested in solving problems K, N, and W, as those are the only problems that apply to you, and are the only ones that, if solved, will benefit you. If you were to use the linear approach, assuming you didn't give up right away, you would have to take a long way around, starting with pointless problem "A." (It's interesting to note that the problems whose solutions offer no benefit to you are generally a whole lot harder to solve.) You may spend a lot of time and energy solving a lot of useless problems, not because they will produce any tangible benefit, but because you have been trained to solve problems in a linear fashion.

This is where stupidity can be an enormous help. Here is an example:

There was a woman who wanted to be a published author. She had written an unusual book, and when her manuscript was finished, she went about trying to get it published in what can be called a very intelligent manner: she went to a bookstore and bought every book there was on how to get published.

She proceeded to read all of these books, and she became very well versed on all the methods they preached. She followed the instructions to the letter, with extreme diligence. She spent hours writing beautiful letters to literary agents, asking them to consider representing her book. Her first few letters to agents were met with rejection, but she was not deterred. She continued to look through the listings of agents, and she very methodically continued to write letters every week. She was certain that if she took the exact same linear approach that she had learned in school, and just kept at it diligently, she would find an agent willing to represent and sell her book.

Unfortunately, in spite of all of her best efforts, and in spite of spending hundreds of hours and over three hundred dollars on stamps, in the end all she had to show for all her work was a big pile of impersonal rejection letters.

At this point she was stuck. Even though she had carefully sought out professional advice and had followed all the rules, this linear approach, the one that had served her so well in school, had gotten her absolutely nowhere. She was completely frustrated. She was a very bright person who had gotten all A's in school and was not used to failure. But one day it finally dawned on her that all this so-called intelligence that she had gathered was worse than useless. It was painfully clear that, by diligently following all the universally available instructions, she had made herself completely *un-unique*. She had become completely indistinguishable from all the many other thousands of wannabe authors who had all read the exact same how-to books. All of this standard advice on how to succeed actually guaranteed failure in such a competitive marketplace.

At this point, since her intelligence had not worked, and since she had become desperate, she decided to do something truly unusual: instead of trying to succeed with intelligence, she decided to try to succeed by using her stupidity.

Now how on earth could one use stupidity to get published? Well, she needed to get past a barrier of gatekeepers who had all told her that she could go no further. How could she get past them? Her solution was brilliant in its use of non-thought.

She decided to imagine herself being too stupid to know that the barrier existed. She pretended that she had never read any how-to books, and that she did not know there were such things as literary agents. This meant she had to do it the "hard way"—that is, on her own. Long story short, she published the book herself.

Even though everyone advised her against resorting to the "vanity press," it was her only chance, and in her case it worked beautifully. She gradually found her "audience" by doing highly unusual (and relentless) marketing that standard publishers never would have done. People started to buy her book. And by the way, she also collected 85% of the sale price of each book. Authors who work through agents and publishers only get 15%, if that.

Once she had the book in print, it was amazing how many unique marketing methods popped into her head. Being "stupid" freed her mind from a disempowering and limited "correct" way of thinking. She used her imagination in all sorts of unusual ways, and last I heard she's still selling books. This approach is succinctly expressed in

Principle #22:
Sometimes, Ignoring a Problem
DOES Make it Go Away All by Itself.

Sure, in theory, in a classroom version of becoming a published author, what she did was all wrong. It was dumb. It did not follow the generally accepted known linear system. She made all sorts of mistakes, and so she had to learn many things the hard way. In comparison to the delightful fantasy of having an agent, it was relatively stupid to do all that scut work. But in making herself stupid and doing it "wrong," she freed herself from a rutted path clogged with competition, and she regained complete control of her destiny.

This story also illustrates

Principle #23:
The Choice Is Not Between Being Smart or Dumb. The Choice Is Between Being Effective or Ineffective.

Intelligence is not a guaranteed path to success. Intelligence is a tool that can either help you or hurt you. Like any tool, it works well in some situations and is useless in others. When it comes to achieving your goal, the elements of desire, perseverance, and imagination are far more important than knowledge or intelligence. In fact, all too often, when you try to do something new, intelligence becomes a detriment, as it gives a false promise of easy success. Worse, that false promise of easy success makes your first (inevitable) failure seem so much worse than it is. Intelligence also encourages quitting, because it is an active conspirator in your rationalization and acceptance of failure.

If, on the other hand, you're too dumb to know your goal is impossible to achieve, and you have no expectation of getting it right the first time, and you have no "intelligence" telling you it's ok to quit because it was impossible anyway, you are less likely to give up. Ergo, if you use stupidity, you are far more likely to succeed.

"The most exciting phrase to hear in science, the one that heralds new discoveries, is not 'Eureka!' but 'That's funny'."
                                        –Isaac Asimov

"The majority of successful new inventions or products don't succeed in the market for which they were originally designed."
                                        –Peter F. Drucker

Stupidity and Goals

The infinite amount of what you don't currently know or understand is a vast and often overwhelming concept. Because of this, it is of course a good and practical thing to occasionally limit yourself to just a little piece of it. If you don't do that, you might float about forever and never get focused on anything. Tools like "to do" lists, along with the creation of short- and long-range goals, are a very good way to limit the scope of your perceptions into do-able sizes.

Of course, the trouble with such scope-limiting techniques is that they are, by definition, limitations.

Yes, on the pro side, having a specific goal focuses your energies on a concise path. But there is also a big con: There is often a vague feeling that, if one reaches a certain goal, there will not be any meaningful life experience beyond it. This often has the effect of being a considerable disincentive for actually reaching the goal.

Some people purposefully never really try to attain their primary goal in life, for fear that it might not actually offer the fulfillment that they hope it will. By never reaching it, they avoid that possible disappointment.

And of course there's also the problem of sincerely trying to reach a goal, and yet still failing. What do you do then?

Again, this is where acceptance of the infinity of what you don't know can be so helpful. This is expressed in

Principle #24:
For Every Goal You Can See,
There Is Another One That You Can't See.

There are many famous people who had very specific goals in mind. However, as they approached their goals, they made fairly sizable adjustments. Just to give you a few examples:

Xerox machines were originally designed to make *single copies* of outgoing business correspondence. It was only when everyone in the offices at Xerox started sneaking in to use the first-ever prototype copy machine to make multiple copies of yard sale flyers that the designers woke up to other possibilities.

Alexander Fleming was doing some experiments and forgot to clean out a petri dish that had a bacteria culture growing in it. When he came back from vacation, he discovered that some mold had also grown in the dish, and the mold had killed the bacteria. You may have heard of this failed experiment/ mess in his sink. It's called penicillin.

Ray Crok's original goal was to sell milkshake-making machines to some guys named MacDonald. He gave up on that goal, and instead bought their restaurant and franchised it. I assume you have heard of . . . MacDonald's?

There were some medical researchers who were trying to create a drug that would treat angina. The drug they came up with was a miserable failure, angina-wise. But it had an interesting side effect. You may have heard of this failed heart drug. It's called Viagra.

Yes, these people had goals, but on their way to trying to meet those goals, they saw something new, and redefined their goals. Many people have failed at innovation because their intelligence focused them too tightly on their original goal. If any of the people mentioned above had doggedly limited their thinking to their original goal, their greatest successes would not have happened. Instead of focusing on an idea they already had, they allowed for the possibility of something that they had never thought of before. In every case they ended up doing something a whole lot bigger than what they had originally planned.

"The defect in the intelligence test is that high marks are gained by those who subsequently prove to be practically illiterate. So much time has been spent in studying the art of being tested that the candidate has rarely had time for anything else."

—C. Northcote Parkinson, in Parkinson's Law

Stupidity and Tests

Some people love tests. Others hate them. Whatever your opinion, the fact is they remain as a primary element of institutional education. With few exceptions, just about every school lives and breathes quizzes and tests. The official "ranking" of your intelligence is often defined by how well you perform on tests, so it's important to consider their impact.

First of all, far from being just a benign form of progress-monitoring, tests have a considerable influence on the development of our perceptions. The ultimate effect of tests is to limit your thinking, not to expand it. For example, in a testing environment, students often learn to read assigned books with a "test defense eye;" that is, rather than trying to really grasp the overall experience that the writer of a classic novel is trying to impart, or just enjoy the stories, students will save themselves time and trouble (and limit their perceptions and thinking) by reading defensively, that is, they scan for items that might appear as a question on a test. By scanning for testable information (e.g., characters' names), one could perhaps "prove" that one has read *Moby Dick* without actually having read it.

If the sole purpose of a class is to pass the test, that purpose severely skews what people discuss in the class, as only certain dimensions of a topic can be turned into a test question. A lot of interesting stuff gets left out. Due to Principle #5 (Fear of Looking Stupid Is an Enormous Force), avoiding the shame of failing the test, or giving a wrong answer, becomes the most important element in the process. On many tests, the subject matter is actually moot. It's often a test of your attendance, your willingness to do boring assignments, and most of all, your ability to take tests. Sometimes, if you look at a test the right way, you can discern the answers just by figuring out how the test maker has formulated the test. It's amazing how often test-makers will add hints to the test to make it easier to pass it. Some people are able to pass tests without studying at all, because to them, taking a test is like solving a crossword puzzle, or breaking a code. This has become a sort of academic sub-specialty; there are now web sites that explain how to use statistical analysis to pass multiple-choice tests.

Even for all of that, perhaps the worst aspect of testing and its effect on perceptual skills is how a test will mark off a teensy weensy little piece of the universe and call it "correct," and everything outside of that little box is labeled "incorrect." In test culture, all new ideas are outside the realm of the known correct answers, and are therefore incorrect. By placing so much emphasis on knowing what is already known, test culture tends to limit our ability to see or cope with the infinity of the unknown.

To access the infinite, one must depart from the safety of always parroting back the expected answer. You must be able to accept the risk of being labeled "stupid" if you are to be truly innovative.

Principle #25:
Tests Only Measure Your Ability to
Take the Test You Are Taking.

Principle #26:
The Correctness of an Answer to a Question Is Never Absolute and Is Always Affected by Who Is Giving the Test.

*　　*　　*

One nasty side effect of test culture is so common, so insidious, and so ubiquitous that people seldom notice it.

When you study for tests, the goal is to remember as many little pieces of data that you can. Students will often stay up all night "cramming" for tests, in hopes of storing (in short term memory anyway) as much of these little pieces of data as possible.

Unfortunately, what is not taught is how to "debrief" oneself from a test-cramming experience. Extraneous data takes up synaptic space that could be used for more important things. One of the most important elements of success in any field is the ability to focus your mind. Having stray bits of useless information floating about in your brain interferes with focus, so after you have "learned" all this information, how do you unlearn it? Once the test is over, how do you get rid of this now useless information?

The answer is actually fairly simple. Like so much of stupidity science, the issue is not how to do it. The answer lies in Principle #10, i.e., the answer is simply to permit yourself to do it—or as is so often the case, permit yourself to *not* do it.

You have the option, choice, and freedom to forget anything you want. Like the foreign language phrases you learned for your vacation last year, if you don't actively use and repeatedly review the information, it will simply fade away. If you don't allow your fear of "looking stupid" to make you repeatedly review and renew your collection of useless information, that information will eventually disappear, freeing your mind for more important and useful activities.

Give yourself permission to think and do less.

*   *   *

Here is another test-related issue for you to consider:

Let's suppose that you are taking a test, and there are two questions for you to answer. Now let's suppose that you only know the answer to the first question. This means you will only get a "50" score, which means you will fail the test. Also, let's say the person sitting next to you only knows the answer to the second question, so that person is doomed to fail the test as well.

Now . . . instead of both of you failing the test, let's suppose that the two of you decide to consult with one another and share information. If you do that, both of you will be able to answer both of the questions, and therefore both of you will pass with flying colors.

"Aha," you might say, "but that would be *cheating*."

Yes, this would be cheating, but that is only because in the typical test environment, you are arbitrarily forbidden to utilize this obvious option of highly effective teamwork. If you were to break or remove that rule, superior results would be achieved.

The real question here is not whether cheating is right or wrong. Of course, if you agree to a preset group of limitations, then you should stick to them, otherwise the three-legged race would not be very much fun. However, the arbitrary limitations of a given situation–e.g., taking tests in an academic setting–do not necessarily apply to every other situation. What constitutes "cheating" in one environment may constitute a highly effective collaboration in another. It all depends on what rules you have collectively agreed to beforehand.

Unfortunately, since we consistently use the "individual effort" model in most testing environments, that tends to become the default approach to everything later on.

This immense emphasis on being judged on your individual effort often runs counter to the need for teamwork in the real world. Many people are taught that teamwork is actually immoral, as they have been repeatedly told that asking for help or working collaboratively on solving a problem is "cheating."

This is yet another situation where having superior "intelligence" (i.e., the ability to score well on tests) can be a considerable disadvantage. Those who score well on tests are repeatedly rewarded for working individually, competitively, and non-cooperatively. They also observe others being punished for not following that paradigm; as a result, they come to believe that working cooperatively, even if it gains superior overall results, is inherently wrong. Those with "average" intelligence are much quicker to accept a team approach, which generally gains a better collective result for the participants in the long run.

While a rule against "cheating" on a specific test (i.e., a rule against getting outside help in addressing a problem) may have its unique applications and advantages, one should always remember

Principle #27:

Cheating Means Breaking the Rules, and Different Games Have Different Rules.

                    *   *   *

One of the most insidious effects of tests in general has to do
with its embedded concept of the possibility of "a perfect score."
This sounds wonderful at first, but when someone regularly
receives "perfect scores" on tests, it is easy for them to assume
that the same perfect results can be obtained in real life. This is
an unreasonable expectation.

Seeking perfection sounds great, but all too often it is really just
an example of what is known as "toxic idealism." In practical
terms, it leads to failure and disappointment every time.

The idea of perfection induces a pleasant state of mind. It is also
a laudable ideal. However, it is not a laudable goal, any more
than it is laudable to seek the pot of gold at the end of the
rainbow. It's just not practical. You can't get there, for the
simple reason that it doesn't exist outside the imagination.

All too often, people will hesitate to act, and will wait and wait
for the perfect job. They will hesitate to market themselves or
their products invention until they are perfect. Big mistake. The
state of "perfection" never arrives.

Perfect score dogma has a corollary in "zero tolerance." Don't
you think it odd that the *total lack of tolerance* is so often touted
as good thing? It is rooted in the notion that perfection can be
expected from human beings. Again, great theory, impossible
reality. From a managerial perspective, accepting the
impossibility of perfection makes it easier to patiently accept and
engage in the next best thing, which is a never-ending battle for
constant improvement.

Repeatedly giving your best students perfect scores sends an
interesting message. Praise is good, but if they have achieved
"perfection," where and how can they seek to improve?

On a purely emotional level, part of the appeal of "perfect scores" is the idea that, if one can remove all imperfections, one will be immune from criticism, and no one can insult you or tease you any more. There is also the common belief that if you remove all imperfection, you will immediately attain a state of blissful universal connectivity. Again, this is not only an illusion, it is the exact opposite of reality; if you were to become perfect, people would be obsessed with finding an imperfection in you (if you doubt this, read any celebrity tabloid). Further, if you were a perfect human being, you would be the only one, and you would no longer belong to the massive club of imperfect people who dwell on this planet.

Embrace your imperfect inner idiot.

Fighting Fire with Stupidity

Perhaps you have found yourself in this oh so unpleasant situation: you are in a plane or in a waiting room, and you are stuck sitting next to someone who is just incredibly boring. And we're not talking about the garden-variety-uninteresting-says-nothing boring. We're talking about the talks-and-talks-about-themselves-endlessly kind of boring.

In this situation, most people inadvertently make their problem worse by accidentally invoking the power of the Principles of Applied Stupidity. Many people assume that if they just sit there in silence, and simply ignore or disregard this boring person, that this boring person will eventually "get the hint" and stop talking.

Unfortunately, in almost every case, the opposite occurs. The person just goes on talking and talking. This is because, by your emulating stupidity, i.e., by creating a sort of mental and sonic vacuum, you are drawing that person's energy to you. When you find yourself in this situation, you would be much better off if you were to be intelligent. You can do this by simply stating every random bit of well-known, generally accepted conventional wisdom you can think of. This will make this dull person think that *you* are incredibly boring, and they will quickly become silent in hopes that *you* will shut up.

I realize you don't want to be thought of as an inconsiderate boring person in general, but if you can achieve a positive result with it, why not fight fire with fire? The Principles of Applied Stupidity are all about using things normally thought of as bad to achieve wonderfully positive results. As Machiavelli said, "the end justifies the means."

"Nobody Knows Anything."

> *—William Goldman, Academy Award winning screenwriter, speaking on the ability of Hollywood executives to predict what movie project will succeed.*

The Wizard of Oz Syndrome

You have probably seen *The Wizard of Oz* at least once . . .

If you haven't, well, it's a story of Kansas farm girl who believes in a far-off and fabulously wise wizard who will solve all of her problems. When she actually meets up with him, she discovers that he is not so wise after all. In the end, she has to solve all of her problems by herself. Bummer.

Right up to this shocking ending, and throughout her amazing adventures, Dorothy exhibits one of the most common tenets of smartist culture, which is the earnest belief that all knowledge has been found, and is available from someone else, somewhere else. There is no point in relying upon yourself to solve a problem, as again, there is someone else, somewhere else, who has already figured it all out. And by the way, they can do everything ten times better than you.

It is extremely common for people to believe in the existence of a mythical wizard, one who possesses far greater knowledge and intelligence, that lives somewhere over the rainbow. In fact, it is so common to so many people, that it is now referred to as the *Wizard of Oz Syndrome*.

Why is this syndrome so common? For one thing, it's because

the existence of a Wizard of Oz, or perhaps a similar wise old man on the mountain, is a very pleasant idea. It combats our general fear of uncertainty. (Of course, if such a person existed, he would HAVE to live up on a mountain, as everyone in town would be sick of him making them feel inferior.) While the desire for the wise old man on the mountain has not changed, he has been replaced in the mythological lexicon. Nowadays, he typically takes the form of a research scientist, working deep in the bowels of a large university laboratory (in a town at least 75 miles away). Other than that, it's basically the same idea.

The Wizard of Oz Syndrome is of course highly reinforced in childhood. Up to a certain age, pretty much everything you want or need to know *is* known by someone else, and your days are spent acquiring this seemingly endless pile of pre-existing information.

However, once we become adults, things get a little dicey. Life is no longer a simple proposition, and in the constant turmoil and vicissitudes of life, we wax nostalgic for that childhood state wherein mom and dad, or their wizardly surrogates, knew all the answers and could solve any problem.

The Wizard of Oz Syndrome is a very comforting fantasy state, but it has one major drawback: If you believe there are people out there who know all the answers, you will inevitably (and unfavorably) compare yourself to these imaginary far-off superior people. When you try to do something yourself, you will feel inadequate in comparison to these fantastic characters living in your intellectually inflated, prejudiced fantasy. This fervent belief, that we can never come up to some distant arbitrary standard no matter how hard we study and work, really eats away at our self-confidence.

Just to offer one example, many people have a terrible fear of public speaking. One of the reasons people have this fear is that they are convinced that the audience is sitting in judgement of them, and can see their every flaw and mistake. If you have allowed yourself to indulge in the Wizard of Oz Syndrome, and you are projecting this distant ideal of higher intelligence onto your audience, well of course, you are imagining them to have tremendous power over you, and so of course you are going to be nervous.

But if you reverse this idea and embrace, not only your own inner idiot, but also the inner idiots of everyone in the audience, well, okay, you will have to give up the fond fantasy of greater intelligence existing outside of yourself. But at that point, the audience is no longer to be feared. Instead, you realize that, like yourself, they are to be pitied and given sympathy.

There is of course an entire economy based on this ubiquitous human desire to find the wise person on the mountaintop. To meet this demand, all sorts of experts and consultants claim to know the answers to all of our problems. We spend an awful lot of time and money on them. However, sooner or later, just like Dorothy, we must sadly accept the fact that very often, they don't know any more than we do. There are, of course, many people out there who are quite knowledgeable in their field and can help you here and there, but none of them are omniscient. This leads us to

Principle #28:
Even the Smartest People in the World Have Finite Amounts of Intelligence and Knowledge. Their Ignorance Outweighs Their Intelligence by Miles and Miles.

It is always a tough pill to swallow when we realize that a fond childhood belief is not true. We all want to believe in the existence of easily acquired greater wisdom lying just over the horizon. But if we indulge ourselves in that fantasy, nothing else works. Hanging on to that fond illusion demands that we ignore all sorts of obvious facts and weave a tangled web of denial to make it all make sense. Our self confidence takes a tremendous hit too.

At this point it is worth pointing out that, along with an exaggerated belief in external wisdom, Dorothy had an exaggerated belief in external evil as well. The wicked witch, who at first seemed all-powerful, was eventually dispatched with nothing more than a cup of tap water. Dorothy always had the power to get home by herself, but at first she didn't realize it. She had to get rid of her belief in power outside of herself before she could believe in power within herself. That is the real "moral" of the story.

Acceptance of the truth—that most people, however "smart" they try to look, are just as lost as confused as you are about the meaning of life—is a tough part of growing up, but accepting it gives you the power and freedom to just be yourself. Once Dorothy figured this out, she was home in ten seconds.

I Don't Know

If you want to see one of the darkest elements of smartism in action, just try this simple test. Go up to a series of strangers on the street and ask them if they can direct you to a nearby address or landmark.

Of course, some of them will be thrilled to show off their intelligence by giving you the answer to their question, but then . . . watch what happens when someone does not know the answer to your question.

Instead of simply saying "I don't know," most people in this situation will hem and haw and try to come up with an answer. They will play a game of twenty questions with you, to see if they can derive the answer from little hints. They will do this even though you have made it clear that you have no idea of where you are. This is because some people will feel genuinely ashamed when they are asked a question that they cannot answer.

This is a sad state of affairs, and it is a real problem. It's not just because everyone's time is being wasted. It's because there is this common belief that ignorance is shameful, and we must do whatever we can to hide it.

This state of mind is a major barrier to acquiring greater wisdom. How can you learn anything new if you believe that you know everything already? How can you learn anything new if admitting to not knowing the answer to every question is a cause of great shame and embarrassment? And worse, how can you risk asking someone a difficult question? If there is a chance of them not knowing the answer, you risk embarrassing *them*. One starts to believe it's better not to ask any questions in the first place.

All the emphasis on "being smart" has its points, but it also has this cumulative effect: It makes it hard to accept one's infinite ignorance. If someone is unwilling to admit that they don't know something, it is not likely that they are ever going to learn anything new.

So the next time someone asks *you* for directions to a place you have never heard of, don't try to fudge up an answer. You can save everyone a lot of time if you simply refer to

Principle #29:
"I Don't Know" Is an Acceptable Answer.

When Stupidity and Intelligence Meet

If you are a fan of the original *Star Trek*, you will recall how Captain Kirk had to match wits with many adversaries. Along with the many human and alien bad guys (and girls) he had to face, some of the bad guys were . . . computers.

These bad-guy computers would be incredibly powerful. They knew everything, and they could do anything. They would often be in charge of entire planets, or they would be roaming around loose, threatening the existence of all life in the universe. Everyone would be all upset, and Captain Kirk and his crew would run around for fifty-five minutes trying to figure out what to do about it; but no matter what they did, it always appeared to be impossibly dire, because these computers were always so much smarter than the human good guys.

Then, at the very end, Captain Kirk would ask the computer a simple question. It would be a question that had no logical or knowable answer, like, "Okay, Mr. Computer, if Pluto is a Dog, then what's Goofy?" Without fail, a few seconds later, in a massive burst of infinite logarithmic calculations, the computer would overheat and blow up. The End. Roll Credits.

When I was a teenager, this always seemed like a grand bit of typical Captain Kirk genius/heroics, but in retrospect, this really wasn't all that impressive. Captain Kirk won out over the computers every time because he understood

Principle #30:
When Smart Meets Dumb, Dumb Always Wins.

Let's illustrate this principle with a more terrestrial example: have you ever encountered someone whose job was extremely simple, like a ticket-taker or a security guard, and you had an unusual or extremely complicated problem that required some special dispensation? And even though this gatekeeper person had no more than a third-grade education and you have something like a doctorate in chemical engineering, how often were you able to get past them? Not very often. All they have to do is ignore you and/or do nothing, and they win.

Intelligence requires energy. Stupidity does not. That's why, in a head-to-empty-head contest, intelligence inevitably poops out and gives up, and stupidity always emerges victorious.

Granted, if you are smart, you can sometimes *get around* a dumb person, but you cannot go *through* that dumb person. This is because, in a direct one-to-one confrontation, stupidity is far more powerful than intelligence. Intelligence is finite. Stupidity is *in*finite. When they meet, there's no contest.

Also, intelligence, by its nature, leaps around and changes constantly. Dumb does not. Dumb is like the fenceposts in a slaughterhouse pen. The fenceposts are as dumb as . . . a post. And it is the intelligence of the cattle, however meager, reacting to the immovable fenceposts, trying to find a way around them, that puts the cattle in the chute. The cattle are convinced of their intellectual superiority over the fenceposts right to the very end.

The "stupidity emulation" that has been discussed throughout this book can be very powerful and effective, but in this case we are talking about something a little different. Here we are talking about something even more powerful. This is not about a slow thought, a half-baked thought, or a poorly constructed thought. This is about the use of *pure* stupidity, i.e., the total lack of any thought whatsoever.

The absence of mental activity is not necessarily bad. It all depends on your point of view. However, for good or for ill, such a state is inert, and you cannot do anything with it, for the simple reason that there is nothing there to do anything with. So when you encounter someone who is either naturally mentally inert or is smart enough to emulate such a state, be careful. Like Captain Kirk's computer adversaries, the more you try to understand nonsensical thought, or worse, the more you try to counter a total lack of thought with your intelligence, the quicker your mental circuits will overheat and explode.

The human mind is designed to investigate, trouble-shoot, and problem-solve, and when we encounter something that is nonsensical, our first response is to think harder. This is a huge mistake. The computers in those classic *Star Trek* episodes were programmed to think a lot and be smart. What they did not understand is that there are times when you are much better off simply not thinking, as thinking about an unsolvable problem will eat up all your energy in an endless pursuit of something – i.e., *sense*– that in many situations simply does not exist.

Lack of sense, logic, or thought is a tough force, which is one of the reasons why we curse it so vehemently. If you cannot easily go around it, do not make the mistake of thinking you can directly overcome it with cleverness. You are much more likely to overcome it with even more stupidity.

Just to give you one sad example of my own experience with this power:

It takes a lot of intelligence to become a member of a symphony orchestra. Years of lessons and training are required to become versed in a 500-year-old tradition of playing music that is mostly over 100 years old and must be played the way "it is supposed to be played." And of course playing in an orchestra, especially a string section, is a study in conformity.

136

Yet within highly intelligent orchestral culture, there is a common stereotype about the relatively lower intelligence of percussionists. This is illustrated in jokes about drummers, all of which make fun of their supposed general feeble-mindedness (e.g., "What do you call a drummer without a girlfriend?" Answer: "Homeless.")

This stereotype of drummers being the "dumbest members of an orchestra" is rather interesting when you note that percussionists, by and large, are usually the wealthiest members of any orchestra. You will often see them during intermissions on their cell phones, managing their real estate empires, or making sure their drumstick factories are up and running.

I once had to hire an entire symphony orchestra for a recording job. Along with all the strings, brass, and woodwinds, I also had to hire a percussionist.

At the end of this job, I paid everyone for their time, but a few days later, I received a bill from the percussionist. It turns out his tympani were in use at some show downtown. He had to rent another set of tympani for my project, and he expected me to pay for the rental. He also expected me to pay for the cost of hauling his instruments to and from the job.

Now bear in mind, all the other players in the orchestra brought their own instruments along, at no extra charge. Some of them had brought violins worth over a quarter of a million dollars. Other than this percussionist, no one expected to get a rental fee for their instruments, or for hauling their instruments to the job. And yet, here I was being asked to pay this percussionist three times as much money as anyone else, for maybe a tenth as many notes.

So I phoned this percussionist and tried to calmly and logically discuss this issue with him. I could see paying "cartage" (as it is called in the business), as percussionists have to bring so much stuff, but paying rentals for instruments, this I could not understand—so I made the mistake of trying to argue with him. I tried every avenue, including logic, precedent, and common sense. I made what I felt were brilliant arguments for my side, thinking I would eventually win him over.

After about 20 minutes of this, I was totally and utterly exhausted. In the same time period I think he had answered 30 emails and fulfilled a few thousand dollars worth of orders from his percussion supply business. Where our conversation was concerned, he made no effort to think, argue, or present logic. All he repeatedly said was, "Sorry, but that's our policy." He gave me a dull, endless, unenergetic, unchanging, unthinking response over and over again until I was completely worn out.

I thought I was completely in the right, and yet his stupidity—his dull, relentless, total inaction of mind—completely overwhelmed my best intellectual efforts.

I finally decided it was not cost-effective for me to continue the discussion. I realized, too late, that I had tried to defeat dumb with smart. I never had a chance.

Because stupidity is infinite, and intelligence is finite, you can never hope to overcome the power of stupidity with mere intelligence. You can use intelligence to *avoid* stupidity, you can use intelligence to *go around* stupidity, but you cannot use intelligence to *defeat* stupidity, for stupidity is an insatiable black hole of non-energy that consumes all intelligence that touches it, and still demands more.

True, you can occasionally "outsmart" someone, but outsmarting someone implies that the person you outsmarted is also somewhat intelligent, just slightly less so. Fair enough. If smart encounters smarter, smarter will usually win. And we often rely upon the ubiquitous fear of looking stupid to force our opponents into a battle of wits, where we have a chance of winning. But no matter how brilliant you may be, when you encounter dumb (and it only has to be average, basic, garden variety dumb), dumb always wins.

You may have avoided using this power because you have been taught all your life that stupidity is bad. It's not good or bad, it's just a tool, and if you understand how it works, you can use it for your own benefit. For example, in retrospect, I should have just repeatedly said to the percussionist that "this is MY policy," and let him try to get around *my* fenceposts of stupidity.

That would have been my only chance. It might have worked, but I have to say, while it is fairly easy to outsmart a violinist, it is very hard to out-stupid a percussionist.

"Do not trust to your 'reason' when creating your plan for accumulating money . . . Your reason is faulty."
        –Napoleon Hill, in "Think and Grow Rich."

Stupidity and Desire

One of the great misconceptions promulgated by smartist culture is the notion that success comes about entirely as a result of being smarter. Being smarter may be helpful, but the real key to success is not about being smarter, or even from having more education, connections, or talent. While these attributes are certainly handy and may occasionally lead to success, the greatest cause of success, more than any other, is desire.

This is not a new idea. Napoleon Hill describes this technique in his classic success book, *Think and Grow Rich*. However, while many people talk about "going for your dreams," not enough time is spent on eliminating the things that may stop you from making those dreams come true. All too often, too much intelligence is one of those things.

The idea that one should seek success via cleverness, rather than via desire, bases its claim on the greater virtue of efficiency, i.e., that one should try to find a quick and easy way to success rather than using a grinding relentless approach. This sounds good in theory, but in practice it is a sure-fire way of becoming exploited by those who are driven by desire. If you do not develop and act on your own desires, you will forever be directed by those who do. Instead of looking for ways to be rewarded for doing less, if you truly desire something, you will actually take joy in working at it constantly, during every waking hour. A vacation will be torture for you, retirement will be unthinkable, for it will

140

take you away from the thing that you most earnestly desire, which, in most cases, is providing meaningful service to others.

Most people don't realize that the emotion of desire, not rational thought or intelligence, is the one true defining element in their lives. Once you are over 21, wherever you are, and whatever you are doing, it is all the result of your own desire. Granted, you may have lousy desires–for example, your greatest desire may be to please your parents, impress your neighbors, or "fit in" . . . but in every case, your actions follow your desires.

If you desire something beyond what you currently have, greater knowledge and intelligence will occasionally be useful in achieving your desires, but all too often, too much thinking complicates matters, adds extra unnecessary steps, and slows the process. For example, if you want "this," but if your intelligence tells you that you need a degree to get what you want, you may have added an unnecessary step. The attendant frustration and delay might become so painful that you are led to suppress your true desire rather than act upon it, or you might start to believe that you are not "smart enough" to achieve your goal, and you will unwittingly allow that negative shaming thought to suppress the positive force of your desire.

This, more than any other, is the best reason to adopt the Principles of Applied Stupidity. If you do not allow opinions, information, standards, or conventional wisdom to interfere with your core desire, and instead you simply move towards your desire, success is far more likely.

In school you learned to follow procedures designed by other people. You learned to become more aware of other people's desires, and less aware of your own. Enormous pressure was placed upon you to pay attention to the desire of the group. What you learned in school was mostly to suppress or subvert your own desires to the desires of someone else.

If you indulge your own desires, and they are contrary to someone else's desires, there is a strong possibility that your desires will be labeled as "stupid."

That's okay. Embrace your inner idiot. He's the only one you can trust, because he is too stupid to ever lie to you.

Doom and Gloom

One of the biggest problems with smartist culture, and the eagerness to define oneself as "smart" as quickly as possible, is how it encourages pessimism and cynicism.

When you set out on a new venture, invariably, no matter how much planning you do, you will make mistakes. Sometimes those mistakes result in fairly unpleasant consequences. These consequences are unpleasant enough on their own. But after you experience them, there is always a likelihood of smartist culture making you feel worse by telling you that if you had "read the manual" or "consulted with an expert" you could have avoided these unpleasant consequences.

The trouble with this particular brand of smartism is this: it bases its self-satisfaction and importance on the idea that it can predict bad things for just about any potential enterprise. This almost always happens only after the fact, telling you that the bad consequences were foreseeable "had you been smart about it."

Now it is true, the majority of new business startups fail, so there is a good statistical likelihood that if someone predicts failure, in most cases they will be shown to have guessed right. But is this really smart? Of course not. They are, in essence, saying there is no point in trying anything new, since there is a chance of failure in everything.

Yes, there is a lot to be said for looking before you leap. But some people, in an effort to avoid potential unknown unpleasant consequences, spend their whole lives looking and never leaping.

As a wise man once said, "some people spend their lives getting ready to get ready." This eternal hesitancy is often excused, rationalized, and even encouraged as being "smart." But is it?

This aspect of smartism, more than any other, exposes what is really at the heart of it: fear. And it's not just the fear of the failure of the project itself, it's the fear of the embarrassment resulting from a failed attempt at something new, and perhaps also the loss of social standing.

You have to consider just how valuable your non-embarrassment and/or social standing is, vs. what you can gain by risking it. That's a decision everyone has to make for themselves. However, most of the time, the dire consequences that we imagine, i.e., of falling short of expectations and looking stupid, are nowhere near as bad as we think.

You may find that, when you screw something up royally, more often than not, someone you respect and think is really smart will pull you aside and say "that's nothing, let me tell you about how I did something that was much much worse." In fact, doing dumb things yourself lessens other people's fear of losing their own social status, and so by doing dumb things and risking your facade of total brilliance, you are actually making other people feel better and encouraging them to take more of a risk in their lives too.

Almost invariably, when I go off on a new venture and actually have some success at it, people who are eager to have the same success will come to me and ask how I did it. They are generally disappointed when I tell them I did it all by trial and error. Worse, my information is generally useless to them, because they were looking for a failure-free "smart" way of getting the same results. It's often impossible to achieve any meaningful success without risking the occasional bad consequence, but smartism preaches that all bad consequences

144

can be avoided. So if you want to be smart, and we all do, you end up spending an inordinate amount of time planning and planning, and never actually doing.

Trying something new always carries with it a harsh prerequisite: you have to risk discovering that you don't know what you are doing, and fear of looking stupid is an enormous force. Opening up a big empty vat of ignorance in your head is kind of scary, for you can't really predict what is going to fall into it. This is a loss of control, or least a loss of an imaginary sense of control. This loss of control and its attendant feeling of fear is what people think of as dumb. Yes, it is uncomfortable at times, but it is the only way to really grow.

The problem of smartism is that it insists on everyone already knowing everything in advance. It abhors the idea that people can just go off and be allowed to explore, and accept that loss of control.

One of the stupidest people who ever lived was Christopher Columbus, and look at how much he achieved because of it. He openly stated that he thought he could get to the East by sailing West, and yet, despite this apparent lack of basic understanding regarding the operation of a compass, he still got some financial backing. He then sailed off into the sunset, and got completely lost. He never quite figured it out, either. True, he ran into North America, but it's not like he hit a small target. He wasn't really an explorer per se; he was just trying to find a new route to a place other people had already been to. When he saw land, he thought he had found India. This guy never knew where he was going or where he had been, and yet we think of him as a great explorer. Well, okay, maybe he WAS a great explorer, but the only reason he discovered America (or the only reason some guy on a beach in The Bahamas discovered him, depending on your point of view) was because he was not constrained by a shred of intelligence.

145

So the next time you are afraid to start a new project for fear of not having enough knowledge about how to do it, just think back on how old Chris did things and take off. He never made it to where he thought he was going. You really can't do any worse.

"Success is the ability to go from one failure to another with no loss of enthusiasm."
—Winston Churchill

Failure Management Part I

One of the most convoluted, counter-productive, and purely nonsensical aspects of smartist culture is how it deals with the concept of failure.

In the typical context of smartist training, we all want to succeed and be smart, as denoted by getting an "A." And of course we all want to avoid failing and looking stupid, as denoted by the shameful grade "F."

We are generally taught from early childhood to define failure, not just as a less than optimal result, but as an embarrassing situation as well. We associate the word with unbearable feelings of shame and disconnection. As a result, many people live in dire fear of failure.

It's time to take command of your "failures." It's time to undo this learned association, and free yourself from the supposed power of this word. Instead of running for the exits in panic at the mere hint of this particular "f" word, if you simply use the Principles of Applied Stupidity, you can return to sanity. To do this, let's take a moment to examine failure calmly and objectively. We begin with

Principle #31:
Failures are Derived from Arbitrary Standards.

A standard failure consists of two elements:

First, you must have a thing or action that is to be judged as a failure or as a success and

Second, you must have an Arbitrary Standard of Judgement (also known as an ASJ), by which you shall do the judging.

Arbitrary Standards of Judgement may be an unfamiliar concept to you, so here is a little story to illustrate ASJ's in action:

Once upon time there was a guy who was hired as a freelance project manager. It was his first time doing this kind of work, so he was eager to do everything exactly right.

His client asked that he begin by submitting a budget for the project. Once that budget was approved, this guy could go ahead and do the project, and then conclude with the final step of submitting an invoice.

So, not having read this book, this fellow proceeded to do an absolutely brilliant job on the initial budget. He researched, he consulted, he plotted, and eventually he laid out a budget containing a very precise series of highly accurate numbers for all of the many elements of the job.

This absolutely gorgeous budget was submitted to the bean-counter bureaucracy, and it was approved. Next, the actual project began. Everything went swimmingly. It all came together beautifully, and the end result was thrilling to everyone. However, there was one minor flaw: one little unforeseen element had to be added, and the final cost was $500 over the initial budget.

Well . . . even though the project itself was a huge success and had actually been achieved at a very low cost, all sorts of people in the bureaucracy of this company could only see one thing: the invoice was "over-budget." In their view, over-budget projects were the worst thing imaginable. They paid this guy's final invoice, but only after considerable hemming, hawing, and harrumphing about the added expense.

This guy was a little bummed about the reaction of his clients. He had done a really fabulous job for them, but all they could talk about was this one little cost overrun. Phooey.

So anyway, six months went by, and this guy was hired again by this exact same company to do, essentially, the exact same project all over again. Well, you didn't have to hit him over the head with a baseball bat more than once. As before, he did up a budget . . . but this time, he surreptitiously added a 10% contingency into it. Instead of being dead-on accurate, he added little odd amounts . . . here, there, and everywhere . . . making the additional 10% invisible to the naked eye.

The new (slightly cooked) budget was approved, the project was executed, and again it was a big success. And again, just like the last time, there was yet another minor cost overrun, but this time, due to the surreptitiously inflated numbers, instead of the invoice being $500 over budget, it was $1,500 *under* budget.

Now, you might think that people would be upset at the inaccuracy of the initial budget. Nope. No one even looked at it. Instead, everyone praised him to the skies as being a genius. "Wow, you did this whole project and you came in under budget!" They were thrilled.

These two projects were virtually identical, but one of these projects was deemed a failure, and the other project was a big success. Why? The projects were the same, but the *budgets* were different. By applying a different *Arbitrary Standard of Judgement*, one project was thought a failure, while the other identical project was thought to be a success.

What many people fail to notice is that failure doesn't occur in a vacuum. It is never absolute. There has to be a budget, or some other standard, against which a given thing or an action is to be negatively judged. In fact, you can take virtually any activity and say it is a grand success or a miserable failure, merely by moving the budget, that is, the ASJ, this way and that.

When discussing a failure, we tend to focus solely upon "the thing getting judged," so the attendant Arbitrary Standards of Judgement (ASJ's) that cause the perception/labeling of failure rarely get the attention they deserve. Instead, like the cooked budget above, they tend to be accepted without question. They often look like they are written in stone and handed down from on high, but in fact they are fairly ephemeral items. Anyone–including you, me, or anyone walking past–can make up an ASJ any old time they feel like it. You can take anything and call it a failure or a success, merely by changing the *Arbitrary Standard of Judgement*.

There are many different kinds of insidious budgets in your life. Your parents' expectations can be a budget. Your next door neighbor's possessions can be a budget. Your siblings' achievements can be a budget. Any or all of these things can be turned into Arbitrary Standards of Judgement, against which you might unfavorably compare yourself.

In dealing with ASJ's for yourself, it's fine to set goals and standards for yourself, as long as they are reasonable; but always check to make sure the ASJ's floating around in your subconscious are of your own calm and rational choice, and are not a vague general presumption of the community's standards for success.

When other people try to impose an ASJ on you, you can easily

150

counter that with the use of Principle #10. When you understand that these outside ASJ's are there to manipulate you and make you feel bad for not conforming, and they are designed strictly for that purpose and are not a fair or proper objective standard, you can see them for what they are, and either manage them or simply ignore them.

The one simple rule you must always remember about budgets, ASJ's, and failure is this: *you are the only person with the authority to create a "success budget" for yourself and your life.*

*   *   *

One quick addendum: in examining the ASJ's in your environment, you may discover this oh-so-common use (or perhaps mis-use) of ASJ's:

There are many people who espouse exceptionally high ASJ's, consisting of virtually unattainable standards of perfection. When you first encounter such people, you can't help but be impressed. However, while they promulgate these standards for others, and they will harshly judge anything you do in comparison to these high standards, they will rarely (if ever) try to meet these standards themselves in any tangible way. Be careful how much weight you give to such lofty ASJ's, as all too often they are 1) terribly vague, 2) really just a cover for feelings of inadequacy, or worse, 3) a marketing gambit to get you hooked on an endless series of training sessions.

In setting your own ASJ's, be careful to not to do the same thing yourself and automatically default to the highest ASJ imaginable. Idealism is a fine thing, but again, this always risks becoming toxic idealism. It's generally best to avoid a situation in which you are essentially guaranteeing disappointment no matter how hard you work. Set your personal ASJ's high, but no higher than you absolutely have to in order to achieve happiness and success. No point in making life harder than it already is.

Failure Management Part II

Contrary to what you may have heard, no one in their right mind is afraid of failure. What is called "fear of failure" is actually fear of something else. When we don't achieve a hoped-for result, the fact that we are not perfect becomes obvious, and most of us have been conditioned to be afraid of having our imperfect selves exposed to public view.

In your childhood, when you "failed" at something (i.e., you did not meet some authority figure's ASJ), you may have been the victim of people taking that moment of your exposed vulnerability as an opportunity to "dump" on you– that is to say, to express their fear of their own vulnerability being exposed. Rather that embracing the truth of their imperfection, they expressed anger at you for exposing the collective imperfection of the group. Ouch. It is the thought of this painful experience occurring again, not failure itself, that we are so afraid of.

These psychic wounds should of course be taken seriously, but again, the real fear is not fear of failure, it is a fear of being vulnerable, and having that buried trauma or act of abusive behavior reenacted in the here and now. That's a reasonable thing to be afraid of, but once you parse it all out and look at what really happened, the thing you fear has nothing to do with failure, and everything to do with someone trying to conceal the truth. It's time to separate the two ideas.

In managing your own fear of looking stupid, you must also consider the fears that other people have of looking stupid. If someone is responsible for your performance–e.g., a parent or a teacher–and you "fail" to do something as expected, *their* vulnerability is exposed, and *their* buried fears will be brought up to a conscious level. When you were little, you blamed yourself for their pain, and you were very upset over having apparently caused them distress, and that's the awful event we fear occurring again.

Perhaps it's time to require these people to step up, and be more forgiving and accepting of both you and of themselves.

At the very least, always remember to embrace your inner idiot, and while you're at it, you might want to consider embracing some other people's inner idiots as well.

Failure Management Part III

Now that we have established that 1) failure is merely an arbitrary judgement and a theoretical concept over which you have complete control, and 2) by itself it not something to fear, we are ready to consider

Principle #32:
Failure Is Good.

Again, this may surprise you, as we so often think of failure as a sign of stupidity, and as a generally bad thing. But here is the conundrum: as anyone who has succeeded at *anything* will tell you, failure is an ongoing intrinsic element of any meaningful successful enterprise.

Even so, smartist culture preaches and teaches failure *avoidance*. This makes perfect sense in a factory or a bureaucracy, where repetition, efficiency, obedience, and perfection are everything, and your own personal growth is nothing. That approach is now obsolete. To achieve true success, you should think, not in terms of failure avoidance, but the exact opposite: you should embrace failures as a vital intrinsic element of your unique learning process. You must develop skills, not in failure *avoidance*, but in failure *recovery*.

Real success is not the absence of failure. Instead, it is the result of constantly risking failure and doggedly continuing despite a near constant stream of failures. (Here's a bizarre thought for you: "giving up" on something actually ends the prospect of any further failures, so in smartist terms, and in a true semantic corkscrew of the mind, "giving up" is a form of total success.)

The typical academic experience associates failure with shame. There is a very good reason for this: it is a handy means of instilling blind obedience. If you follow all instructions to the letter, a form of minimal "success" (or at least, a lack of failure) is virtually guaranteed. This is fine as far as it goes, but following a philosophy of total failure avoidance creates this problem: If you have had straight A's throughout your academic career, you are, upon graduation, the least prepared of anyone for the real world. This is because when you leave school and enter the real world, you have had no training or experience in handling failure, and handling repeated failure is one of the most important skills to have in seeking real success.

Your classmates who all got C's, D's, and F's were labeled as being relatively "stupid," and yet they were given opportunities to build up their failure callouses. They can now shrug off a failure as if it was nothing. They have experienced failure, and, having seen it, felt it, and repeatedly survived it, they do not fear it, and it does not defeat them. This is a tremendous advantage.

Granted, this all must seem to be awfully odd to hear, since you have been told so often that failure is unspeakably bad. Sure, by itself, no one really enjoys failure, but that misses the point. Failures are the way to achieve success. Therefore, failures (that is to say, momentary, short term failures), even in vast quantities –are good.

It can be very hard to get past the wretched brainwashing of smartist dogma. It may be making you continually ashamed of getting less than a perfect score in anything you attempt. So when you embark on a new project, instead of demanding impossible levels of perfection of yourself, try accepting your inner idiot. Once you apply Principle #10 (Embrace your Inner Idiot), that little "hitch step" of demanded initial perfection is removed. Next, just assume (as is almost sure to happen) that the majority of your initial efforts will result in failure. Now, the worst that can happen has already been dealt with.

(In fact, you can go one step further and apply a brand new Arbitrary Standard of Judgement to your failures, and judge them to be indicative of eventual success, as they show you have begun the tangible "research" phase of your project.)

Once failure probability has been accepted, and even embraced, you can then go about your business, and try new endeavors with a realistic approach. You will no longer labor under the massive weight of expecting to be perfect. You won't be hindered by any pressure to be a total success on your first try. By accepting your stupidity, you get yourself more in touch with reality, for no matter how smart you are, and no matter how carefully you plan, you are still likely to fail on your first time out. And there is an added benefit: since you have accepted the idea that you are an incompetent boob, the slightest little success will thrill you to death, as it is so unexpected.

There are many people who talk about accepting and overcoming failure, but they consistently talk about it in hushed tones and treat it as if it was a shameful necessary evil. This does not get at the core of the problem. Since failure is necessary to success, how can it be evil? Instead of letting your energy be drained away by your fear of looking stupid, why not embrace your inner idiot, and enjoy tackling the fabulous challenge that has been presented to you?

Failures are like dirty dishes. No one likes them, but they are inevitable, so it's kind of silly to be afraid of them. You can avoid dirty dishes, but only if you limit yourself to fast food and TV dinners. Yuck.

Success is good. Momentary short-term failures are an essential element of achieving ultimate success. Therefore, failure is good.

Leadership, Stupidity, and Problem-Solving-Part-II

Consider for a moment just how often you have observed the following behavior:

A small child is being assisted in some task by a solicitously caring parent. The parent ties a shoelace, or successfully resolves some issue with the operation of a new toy. But then, even though everything is now fixed, the child starts to cry.

When the child is asked why they are crying, the child gives this common response:

"I wanted to do it myself."

Another similar situation: You have boarded a plane, and, having forgotten to bring a book, you reach for the airline's in-flight magazine. You turn to the crossword puzzle, and you discover that it has already been filled in by someone else. Now: are you pleased and thrilled that someone else has already done all the work and figured out the puzzle? Of course not. You wanted to do it yourself.

Let's extend this out a little bit. The next time you are walking through an airport terminal, take a look around. You will seldom see anyone just sitting and staring into space. Even though they have the option of doing nothing, most of the people you see will either be doing puzzles (crossword or Sudoku), or they will be playing FreeCell, Minesweeper, or some other electronic game. These people have all freely chosen, and actually prefer, to solve puzzles rather than sit and do nothing.

From these many common occurrences, we can conclude that human beings are incredibly eager to solve problems.

Granted, for various reasons, some people lose faith in their ability to solve their own immediate personal problems, but this does not stop this universal compulsion; it is merely channeled into vicarious problem-solving activities. A quick look at your nightly television program lineup will reveal a limitless offering of armchair problem-solving. Most television "dramas" consist, essentially, of a puzzle that needs to be solved. One oh-so-common example: the show begins with the discovery of a dead body. We will sit there for an hour, through endless commercials, vicariously figuring out the puzzle of "whodunit." And of course most "reality shows" offer the same endless problem-solving activities. We can't get enough of it. Once the murderer is found out, or once the miniseries is finally over and everyone is rescued from the island, we ought to be relieved that the uncertainty has ended, but instead, we are disappointed. We like to be in a state of solving problems.

The issue with problem-solving is not a lack of ability (or desire) to solve problems. The issue is actually an *overabundance* of the ability and desire to solve problems. In fact, this ingrained human propensity for problem solving is so ubiquitous, that many times there are situations where there are far more problem-*solvers* than there are problems to be solved. When this happens, people in positions of highest authority will usually nab the opportunity to solve the puzzles, and not allow any of their underlings to have any of the fun.

This is yet another perfect example of how stupidity can be used to much greater effect than intelligence. In this case, when you find yourself in a position of authority, instead of hogging the pleasure of doing the crossword puzzle all by yourself (and then expecting your underlings to merely execute your solution), consider doing what the best managers do: pass up the pleasure of solving of the problem on your own, and let everyone else participate in, or even take over, the problem-solving process.

On a purely emotional level, this is often very hard to do. Like the kid in the shopping cart, you of course want to do it yourself. Restraining yourself, and letting your child or your employees have the pleasure of solving the problem, will be difficult to do. However, this offers several advantages: for one thing, it gets everyone invested and involved in a way that mere obedience to a someone else's preexisting solution can never do, no matter how good the preexisting solution is. Also, there is a statistical probability that if ten people work on a problem, they are ten times more likely than one single person to come up with a better solution, even if that one person is a brilliant genius, i.e., you.

The desire to look smart, and the attendant ego rush that we all feel when we demonstrate our mental abilities (as demonstrated by solving the problem), is a tough cookie to pass up. The best managers, however, all have the ability to control this urge, and instead they step back and let larger teams work on the puzzle all at once. This is just one of many situations where one can gain significant advantages by employing

Principle #33:
Let Other People Solve the Problem.

*　　　*　　　*

A small addendum to the above:

While the previous chapter was designed for managers and leaders, it is important for the average "managee" to know this Principle as well. This is because you may occasionally find yourself in the not-uncommon position of working for a manager, or dealing with a co-worker, family member, etc., who *does* know and use this principle, and is using it to great effect . . . on *you*.

Be advised: like everyone else, you are born with a natural predilection, even a compulsion, to solve problems. Therefore you may find yourself in situations where people in your environment (again, managers, co-workers, family members, etc.) are abusing their privileges by presenting you with an endless litany of problems to solve, both professional and personal.

Once more, the Principles of Applied Stupidity to the rescue. While it is fun, entertaining, and ego-boosting to solve problems, take care that you do not fall into a state of constantly solving other people's problems for free. Every once in a while, you have the right to say "I do not have to solve this problem." Take a look around and see if other people have discovered that the easiest way to solve every problem is to dump it in your lap.

You are not being noble by taking on every puzzle all by yourself. If you are unilaterally solving every problem or puzzle, it's a good bet that you are really just falling into the smartist trap of indulging your own problem-solving compulsion and ego. Sure, by solving all these problems you are showing all these "dumb" folks how smart you are . . . but are you?

The right thing to do is often referred to as "tough love," and the reason it's so tough is that it is so difficult to restrain our compulsion to solve every problem we see. Sometimes, the best course of action is not to be smart. Sometimes, the best course of action is to sit back and be stupid, and allow others to re-acquire confidence in their own innate problem solving skills.

While it goes against smartist training not to show off how clever you are at all times, sometimes stupidity is the better part of valor.

*　　　*　　　*

Another very important use of problem-solving avoidance (as well as failure acceptance) is in the realm of negotiations.

When you negotiate with someone, in theory, each side makes successive concessions until an equitable middle ground is reached. But here is the problem: if you view a negotiation as a problem that must be solved, you may feel compelled to make as many concessions as necessary to achieve that result . . . perhaps more than your fair share. On the other hand, if you become completely apathetic as to whether the problem gets solved or not, you put your counterpart in the position of having to overcome *their* pressing desire to "solve the problem." If they have not embraced their inner idiot, this puts them at a tremendous disadvantage. If they cannot control their problem-solving compulsion, the only way they can solve the problem is to do it in a unilateral fashion, i.e., to make ever more concessions to you.

In other words, in a negotiation, the person who is most eager to solve the problem . . . loses.

If you have ever wondered why negotiations between nations take so long, it's because the professionals know it's always better to let the other guy offer a solution first. Again . . . *let other people solve the problem.*

*　　　*　　　*

Speaking of the importance of not solving problems:

I once knew a very charming young lady who had an alarming ability to attract men. It was amazing to see just how many men fell madly in love with her on a weekly, and sometimes daily, basis. However, while attracting so many wannabe suitors made

162

for an interesting hobby, the men who instantly fell in love with her had no appeal for her. She was much more interested in the few men who were *not* interested in her.

At first, this behavior on her part may seem to be totally illogical to you. But then you realize that, like all the rest of us, she was a born problem solver. She was only interested in those rare individuals who could (at least momentarily) resist her overwhelming charm. Overcoming that rare resistance gave her something to do.

There is an analogy in the animal kingdom: cats will play with a mouse only as long as the mouse tries to get away. Once the mouse is dead, the cat loses interest; there is no more problem to solve. In relationships and everywhere else, people look to solve problems, and if there are no problems, they will either create them, or leave to go find them somewhere else.

I'm not suggesting that you seek to cause problems in your personal relationships. They will of course occur all by themselves. I *am* suggesting that you should not immediately set out to always solve them unilaterally, for the simple reason that doing so gives the other party little to do all day.

The presence of puzzles, challenges, obstacles, and resistance are key to creating interest, in romance as well as in any workplace. If there is no problem for others to solve, there is no interest. If you shower someone with anything and everything they want, yes, you look to be very generous, but in fact you are denying them one of the primary things that all human beings desire, which is to face and solve a challenge.

If you wish to effectively engage with other people, don't demonstrate a superior ability to solve problems. Embrace your inner idiot, stand back, and offer problems for them to solve.

Part Four:

Tales of Stupidity in Action

Stupidity with a Double Bass

When I was an aspiring young teenage bass player in Ohio, I took bass lessons with a number of well-known university-level double bass instructors. These instructors were all brilliant, no doubt about it. There was nothing about the double bass that these people didn't know. They had all devoted their lives to the art and technique of playing the bass. They had published books and articles, they had formulated theories and methods, and they had all analyzed bass playing to an extraordinary level. Whenever I had a lesson with one of these superstar teachers, I was mesmerized by their knowledge of the double bass.

Unfortunately, since all I could think about was how brilliant they all were, I never got any better myself. I could never imagine myself doing all the many technical feats that they described in minute detail. I felt stupid when I dared to practice for my next lesson, for in the presence of such great teachers I felt like I was nothing. I only practiced in order to not quake in my boots with shame for not having done so. In my heart I felt practicing was pointless, for no matter how much I practiced, I knew these teachers would find, and carefully point out, every little error I was making. I also knew that they would then offer ever more suggestions for improvement, far more than a mere mortal like myself could ever hope to comprehend or implement. There were so many things I didn't know how to do, it all seemed hopeless. I felt that I could never attain such levels of playing myself, no matter how hard I might try. So I didn't. My one solace was I was able to say that I was studying, however pointlessly, with some truly brilliant teachers.

The upshot of all these many lessons was that I became just

another average high school bass player.

When I graduated high school, I was sick of writing term papers, so I decided to go music school instead of college. I wound up taking lessons with a fellow that (to avoid lawsuits) I will call "Uncle Bob." Uncle Bob played the bass in the Boston Symphony. He had a reputation for turning out quite a few highly successful bass players. He had a very liberal policy about who he would accept as a student, so despite my mediocre audition, I found myself studying with him.

I assumed that lessons with Uncle Bob would be similar to my experiences with my previous double bass instructors, but I assumed wrong.

To start, Uncle Bob didn't teach in some fancy well-appointed conservatory studio. Instead, I would take a train to his house in the suburbs, and the lessons took place in his living room. It was a very small room, made ever smaller by the presence of at least 500 figurines of little bass players that were made out of every element in the periodic table, from blown glass to ceramics to wrought iron. In taking the lesson you had to fit yourself in between the TV set, the ottoman, and the fireplace pokers. One could hear his wife rattling pots and pans in the adjoining kitchen, louder or softer, depending on their level of marital conflict that day.

Lessons with Uncle Bob were something of a communal affair. Anyone who happened to be around would sit in on them, including friends, neighbors, visiting relatives, other students, the mailman, or Pinky, Uncle Bob's poodle.

But even with all the many oddities of the physical environment, these were nothing compared to the presence of the man himself. Uncle Bob weighed something like 400 pounds. He was also a chain smoker and an alcoholic. Other than that, he was in perfect health.

In between his scarfing down some Kentucky Fried Chicken, lighting up a Benson and Hedges 100, and chugging a bottle of creme de menthe, I would play something for Uncle Bob out of a lesson book. However, unlike my lessons with the great pedagogues of the Midwest, Uncle Bob offered no in-depth analysis of niggling little technical issues. Even on those rare occasions when he was conscious enough to articulate actual words, all he would say is, "Sounds great. Play some more." It didn't matter how I played anything. I could screw up royally or play reasonably well. In either case, I always got the same somewhat semi-comatose slurred speech response: "Sounds great. Play some more." There were times when he actually watched television during the lessons.

In spite of this somewhat unorthodox environment, not knowing what else to do, I went through the same motions at these lessons that I had with my previous teachers—or at least I tried to. Each week I would put in the bare minimum amount of practicing required of me, then I would dutifully and obsequiously come in to each lesson expecting to hear a concise inventory of my personal deficiencies. I also assumed that, as in past lessons with other teachers, this would be followed by a lengthy lecture on various technical methods to be used to fix them. I waited patiently, but this never happened. All I heard, week after week, was "Sounds great. Play some more."

This went on ad nauseam every Saturday morning for about a year before I finally said to myself, "Hey—this guy is an idiot. I'm never going to learn anything from him. Sure, he plays in the Boston Symphony, but if someone this dumb can do it, how hard can it be?"

And so I started to practice in an entirely different way. I wasn't sure how I was going to do it, but at this point I was quite certain that, pathetic though I may have been, I could certainly be at least as good—or at least, not quite so pathetic—as one current member of the Boston Symphony Orchestra.

At the time, I thought Uncle Bob was pretty stupid. But now I know he was not as dumb as he looked. He was using the Principles of Applied Stupidity.

Instead of overwhelming me with information, he did the opposite. By playing the role of dumb observer, he created an intellectual vacuum. Even though I did my best to avoid having to make the effort of filling it up myself, he outdid me at every turn. His emulated stupidity had no limits. It was not uncommon, after playing that week's assignment, to look up and discover that Uncle Bob had fallen asleep. He was not going to fill the air with any of his own intelligence. By emulating total stupidity, he succeeded where all my other brilliant teachers had failed. By "out-stuping" me, he forced me to fill that intellectual vacuum on my own, with information of my own making.

In retrospect, before meeting up with Uncle Bob I had, without knowing it, become an expert in stupidity emulation myself. In my past lessons, and in many other so-called learning environments, I had learned how to look and act both pathetic and dumb, thereby creating an informational vacuum. All of my previous teachers had fallen into my little trap; they would always step right up and fill that vacuum with lengthy displays of their own knowledge. I saved myself a huge amount of work simply by keeping my mouth shut and letting them have the pleasure of believing they were smarter than me. (It's amazing just how many students use this technique without even knowing it.)

The difference with Uncle Bob was that, by pre-emptively emulating total stupidity himself, he reversed the roles of who was "smarter." He forced me to take charge of the situation and actually look at my deficiencies myself.

For the first time in my life, I had found myself in a situation where I was not encouraged to make someone else look relatively smart by my looking relatively dumb, i.e., by failing. Once I stopped feeling obliged to be the "dumber" person, my thinking was no longer limited by a belief that I had to completely conform my thoughts to someone else's view of the world. My mind was no longer concerned with what Uncle Bob (snore cough cough) might think, for, in Uncle Bob's emulated total stupidity environment, it was blatantly obvious that listening to him was a total waste of time.

Once I realized that Uncle Bob had no interest in trying to look smarter than me, the whole polarity of the flow of intelligence and information reversed. Instead of looking for all information outside of myself, I discovered (much to my amazement) that I had a virtually infinite capability *inside* of myself to recognize, analyze, and solve just about any technical problem I had. It is truly astonishing just how quickly a total change in my playing manifested itself.

A year later I was playing with the Boston Pops.

Some people think I'm talented. I'm not. I just happened to be the beneficiary (or the victim) of the Principles of Applied Stupidity. They removed all the limitations that existed in an intelligent environment. They maximized my potential, and that beats talent any day. This is just one more example of how stupidity can work wonders where intelligence and careful thought have no chance of succeeding.

Pas de Duh

When big famous ballet companies go on tour, they take along all the dancers and the sets. However, to save money, in each city they typically hire local musicians to sit in the pit and play the music–at least this was the case when the Royal Ballet of London came to Boston on a world tour. They hired me, and some 60 of my colleagues, to play in the pit for their performances.

They had of course brought along their own conductor, and this conductor was absolutely fabulous. We had just two rehearsals with him before the first show, and so he had to get us up to speed in a hurry. He did this in a most unusual way: At the beginning of the second rehearsal, he said to us very quietly, "I have a terrible confession to make." Well, of course, as you know, terrible confessions are always very attention grabbing, so we all became very quiet and leaned forward to hear what he had say.

And he very softly and seriously said, "I am tone deaf."

Well, after working with this guy through one rehearsal already, it was obvious to all of us that he was a master musician, and there was no way that he was tone deaf. So we all just laughed.

Then he continued: "But if you play on the wrong place," he said, "I can hear that. So whatever you do, don't play in the wrong place."

This all may seem ridiculous at first glance, but in fact it was a very tactful way on his part of saying to us, "this is a ballet, and keeping the rhythm right is a whole lot more important than keeping the pitch right." With this little ploy he very effectively conveyed the proper musical priorities to us. There was also this little item added to it: his playful way of claiming that he was largely incompetent led us all to chuckle and say to ourselves, "Well, this poor guy is tone deaf and totally incompetent, I guess we'll all have to step it up and help him along."

It's hard to explain or even believe, but throughout that whole week of performances, we all cranked it up a little bit. Instead of just passively playing the notes and waiting to be told what to do and when to do it, everybody provided an added amount of leadership initiative. The whole event was improved considerably.

It's a strange phenomenon, but when you create stupidity energy, this attracts intelligence. And when you create intelligent energy, it attracts stupidity. I cannot tell you how many times I played for conductors who were incredibly eager to tell us how to play every single sixteenth note. For all of their immense brilliance and the intensely detailed instructions that they presented to us, the net result was a flat perfunctory performance every time, while the guy who openly admitted that he was tone deaf got a fabulous response with minimal time to rehearse.

I admit that this seems counterintuitive, but the empirical data shows the same result over and over again. This is just one more example of the extraordinary effectiveness of the Principles of Applied Stupidity.

Still More Advantages to Looking Stupid

At the risk of being thought terribly politically incorrect, here is a remarkable story of stupidity in action:

There was a kid in my hometown who came from, shall we say, a socio-economically disadvantaged background. He was generally thought of by everyone as being really "dumb." He failed in school all the time. In fact, he failed every grade from sixth grade through his senior year in high school.

When people repetitively fail in school that much, they usually drop out at age 16 or 18. Not this kid. He stuck it out. He kept going and going, repeating every grade, some of them twice, and he did not graduate from high school until he was 26 years old. Everyone accepted this state of affairs. This was partly because this kid just had a "dumb" look about him. It was also because he made everyone else in this socio-economically disadvantaged neighborhood feel at least somewhat superior to *somebody*.

He had few complaints. His life was pretty easy. He rarely did any homework, as he had no real reason to; he had already resigned himself to failing anyway, and he knew he would just have to do the same homework the following year.

At last, he did get his high school diploma, and we can all applaud him for sticking with it and overcoming his stupidity with sheer determination.

However, maybe that's not all there was to it.

Consider the historical context: When this kid finally managed to graduate, the year was 1972. At age 26, he was magically old enough that he was no longer eligible for the draft. While *college* deferments would only keep one out of the draft for a limited time, apparently there was no such time limitation for people trying to finish high school.

The purpose of telling you this story is not to make some sort of political statement. However, it is a simple fact of history that back in those days, a lot of people didn't want to get drafted and go to Viet Nam, and there were many clever methods employed for that purpose. To be honest, I have no idea if this was a purposeful plan on this kid's part, or if it just happened to work out this way; but if his goal was indeed to avoid getting drafted, it was a remarkably innovative and effective use of the Principles of Applied Stupidity.

Another Story of the Power of Stupidity

A few years ago, I met a guy at a party who said he worked for a company that sold home electronics, you know, speakers and stereos and such. He said he was "the head of sound design." I was not very impressed. I am the head of sound design at my company too. Big deal. Anyway, I told him some jokes, he thought I was funny, and long story short, he invited me to come have lunch with him, and see the place where he worked.

Okay, now bear in mind, my default country bumpkin mindset was in high gear here. I had heard of the company he worked at, but this is only because I once had a psychotic roommate who owned a pair of this company's speakers. Lacking any other information, I just assumed that this "speaker company" was a little workshop in a barn. I envisioned a place with sawdust on the floor, where carpenters built speaker enclosures, boxed them up, and hauled them out to the loading dock.

The day for the lunch meeting arrived. This company was in Framingham, and I was not about to get all dressed up for a lunch meeting in Framingham. I threw on whatever was on top of the dresser—in this case, a ratty old wrinkled pair of khaki pants, white socks and sneakers, and a faded polo shirt. I then drove myself out to see what I assumed would be a sincere little workshop with a few carpenters and a guy out in back with a soldering iron.

Well, I got there and . . . oops.

There was no barn, and there was no guy with a soldering iron.

Instead, I found myself staring down the barrel of a major, multi-billion-dollar, Fortune 500 international corporation.

In the beautifully appointed lobby, I was greeted by a Gucci-clad receptionist. I was tersely asked to have a seat in one of the Swedish designer chairs. Seated all around me were various visiting salespeople, all dressed in gorgeous three-piece suits. Like me, they were anxiously awaiting their turn to be allowed into the inner sanctum. But, being dressed as I was, they all looked at me like I was something they didn't want to get stuck on the bottom of their shoe.

It was too late to do anything about this. Changing clothes would have involved an hour's round trip back home, so I swallowed hard and just decided to gut my way through this soon to be oh-so-embarrassing situation.

This receptionist was highly motivated to get me out of her pristine lobby ASAP. She made numerous calls in a not-so-subtle effort to track down my guy and make him come and get me, even though I was early. Very soon after, my buddy showed up to meet me at the desk, and lo and behold, he was wearing a casual cotton shirt and blue jeans. Thank goodness, the "techies" and "creative types" were casually dressed; but even so, their informal garb had a certain fashionable spiffiness that I sorely lacked. I was so mortified about being so woefully underdressed that I didn't say a word about this sartorial elephant in the living room.

Now if you were to look at this situation from a perspective of standard intelligence and logic, you might assume (as I did at the time) that this day was going to end up as a huge disaster. After all, every book on "fashion sense" and "dressing for success" always says to "dress up" for business meetings and interviews.

However, in retrospect, an interesting fact came to light: being so sloppily dressed as I was, this guy and his entire department of creative types looked at me and collectively thought, "Wow—this guy must be really good if he has the confidence to show up here dressed like *that*."

Next thing I knew, I was being introduced to the president of the company.

They couldn't wait to hire me. They became a steady client of mine for years. And incidentally, they offered me top dollar right off, as they just assumed that they had to. After all, if I had been desperate for a job, I would have dressed up, right?

Again, as is so often the case, if I had done things intelligently, correctly, and by the book, I never would have made any sort of impression. I would have looked just like all the other people in that lobby, who, by the way, were all still cooling their heels therein when I left. By doing it all wrong, I stood out from the crowd, and made one heck of an impression.

Stupidity and Relationships

One of the best applications of the Principles of Applied Stupidity is in the realm of relationships. Again, the discovery of the power of stupidity in this realm, as in so many others, came about entirely by accident, i.e., due to actual stupidity. It happened this way:

At my high school there were many beautiful young ladies, but there was one girl whose pulchritudinous presence was simply extraordinary. Her genetic sequencing had resulted in a marvelous rendition of all the slightly exaggerated feminine physical attributes that are extolled in the pages in *Playboy Magazine*. She was a true trophy wife/centerfold in the making, and every heterosexual boy in my class was crazy about this girl. However, amazingly enough, it turns out (and no one except her knew this at the time), she had a terrible social life. This was because every guy in my class just assumed that a girl who was that gorgeous must already have a better offer for a date on Saturday night. No one wanted to be rejected, so no one ever asked her out. She had just transferred from another school, so she had no female friends either; the girls were just as intimidated by her as the boys. She put on a game face, holding her head high in spite of what she felt was a very unfriendly environment. Everyone thought she was "stuck up," but that was a total misinterpretation of her prideful masking of her terrible loneliness. All in all, it was one huge collective misunderstanding based on incorrect assumptions. Everyone thought they were being smart about it, but . . . they weren't.

Well guess what. Enter yours truly, with no brains to speak of. Once I got my driver's license, I was eager to hit the town.

Being a truly shallow young man, I made a list of the girls in my class to call for social engagements. The order of the names on this list was based solely on their comparative sexual allure, so of course, this golden girl was at the top of the list. Unlike the other guys in my class, who possessed some basic social skills, as well as some sense of their own status in the social/sexual hierarchy of high school, I was not handicapped by any such mental activity. I had no information on which to base any such assumptions. I just wanted a date. So I called her up and asked her out. She was in no position to bargain, so guess what? She said "yes."

Now before you get all hot and bothered, for the record, I didn't get all that far. In fact, on our second date, she sicced her family dog on me. But unlike a lot of guys, I can honestly say that I dated the prettiest girl in my high school.

Did I accomplish this through some grand feat of intellectual gymnastics? Was I cleverer than everyone else? No. I did it because I was socially backward, too dumb to know that I wasn't supposed to do it. This story is a perfect example of

Principle #34:
Ignorance of Difficulty = Optimism

In retrospect, I am truly grateful that my competition was so much smarter than me, as that made them freeze up when faced with exceptional circumstances.

Of all the ways that excessive thinking and information-gathering hinders and inhibits decisive action, perhaps the worst one is thinking endlessly about what one will do if one is rejected. How many times have you seen someone running around in mental circles, agonizing over the possible negative consequences of making a request for a date or a job or anything else? This excess mental activity is pointless, because in such situations, the worst thing that can possibly happen is that things will remain exactly the same as they are right now.

"Analysis paralysis" is a common problem. However, in love, career, or any other endeavor, it can be easily overcome, simply by using the Principles of Applied Stupidity.

Part Five:

Stupidity and Leadership

"Brilliant men are often strikingly ineffectual; they fail to realize that the brilliant insight is not by itself achievement."
                                                    –Peter F. Drucker

Leadership and the Unknown

You are always in a leadership position even if you don't think you are. You may be a leader in the standard sense of being a leader of a group of people, but if you aren't, at the very least, you are the leader of your own life.

The application of stupidity in leadership may not seem obvious at first. After all, on paper at least, we always want the "smartest" person we can find to be in charge. We think we want a leader who will always do "smart" things—that is, things we can understand, and things we approve of, but . . .

Stupidity is key to any leadership activity.

If you are to lead, either others or your own life, this means you have to occasionally take charge and initiate action. Some people say leadership is hard, but contrary to what you may have been told, the initial stage of leadership is relatively easy. You probably already know the things you want to do. However, at the same time, you are often prevented from acting freely on these desires by the insidious yet overwhelming pressure upon you to be "smart"—which means you feel obliged to either do it all perfectly the first time, or not do anything out of the ordinary that has not already been done by someone else. The upshot of all this pressure to be smart is that we spend all of our time and energy looking for a way to do things perfectly on the first try. As a result, to avoid looking stupid, we usually end up doing nothing at all.

The need to belong and be accepted by others of our species is a powerful one, and it is primarily this, not a lack of vision or ideas, that will prevent you from being an effective leader. Departing from the norm and/or status quo, especially if there is even a smidgin of risk or unusual expense involved, will immediately be condemned by others (and quite possibly by yourself) as being stupid. It is Principle #5 (fear of looking stupid), not a lack of capability or opportunity, that stymies so many people in their quest for fulfillment.

Your management of the Principles of Applied Stupidity is a key element in taking charge of your organization, or indeed, just your own life. Leading, real leading, implies stepping into unknown territory. It implies risking failure. It implies going into a new environment where you do not know all the rules or all the answers, and you will be making mistakes, probably in full view of other people.

If you want to see a true leadership expert at work, observe any one-year-old child. They have no interest in how they appear to others as they charge into the unknown. They actually welcome the unknown, as their mind, like yours, constantly hungers for new input and information. It is a pleasurable rush to learn and see new things. Yes, infants and toddlers fall down and have booboos, but their rate of intellectual growth is nothing short of astonishing. It is far beyond that of even the brightest adult. They are in a constant state of leading themselves into new situations, both physically and mentally. It is all the "smart" adults who are constantly chasing after them, restraining them and teaching them to conform to outside standards—in other words, suppressing their natural leadership.

This well-intended limitation of your leadership instinct did not end in childhood. It is still going on. People who care about you will forever feel it is their job to protect you by preventing you from exploring too far afield or doing anything new or slightly risky. Granted, children have to be restrained from time to time for their own safety, but this restraint often gets out of hand when we are adults. It gets to the point where all new activity shuts down altogether.

Limited, finite environments are very familiar and therefore very safe, therefore they are smart. New, unlimited, unfamiliar experiences are frightening and outside our comfort zone, and are therefore . . . stupid. So says smartist dogma. So a certain amount of stupidity is inherent in any true act of leadership.

Again, this is where abandoning the supposed benefits of always being in control—of being smart—and inviting disapproval, risk, and loss of control—being stupid—are so essential to your personal advancement.

Eagerness to be smart is what defines a follower, not a leader. Smart followers judge themselves on how well they are conforming to a preset standard. The willingness to do the opposite and risk "looking stupid" defines a leader. Leaders are not sure of the answers, failure is quite possible, and yet they still take the test.

Acceptance of stupidity frees you from spending enormous amounts of energy trying to avoid it, and allows you to get on with the task at hand. Yes, you should of course minimize risks by applying what knowledge you have to predicting possible outcomes, and of course you should do your best to minimize unwanted consequences. But if your goal is to *completely* remove potential bad consequences, you have stopped being a leader. You are waiting for someone else to go ahead of you and call back to you when it's safe.

That may be smart, but it's not leadership.

Leadership and Humility

One of the original purposes of this book was to explain the leadership techniques of the many famous conductors I had the privilege of playing under. Hopefully some of the preceding pages have addressed that goal. But there is one more thing needing mentioning: without exception, the great conductors and musicians I have known all had one attribute in common, and that was massive amounts of humility.

You would think that people at the top of these very competitive professions would be arrogant and condescending, but the opposite was always the case. Of course, it makes so much sense. Those who continually improve are those who are able and willing to continually make honest assessments of themselves.

Despite the power and effectiveness of humility, it is rarely taught. Instead, there is massive emphasis on having pride: in your school, in your heritage, in your country, in your achievements. We associate humility with shame and defeat.

Achievements are just the end result; to truly learn and grow, we must have some mechanism or technique for dealing with the occasional shocking realization that we are nowhere near as good at things as we thought we were. If you can't admit to having a problem, there is precious little hope of your ever solving it. Pride makes you weak. Humility makes you strong.

This is where a departure from smartist culture, specifically, of constantly comparing yourself to others, can be so helpful. If you always think of a learning experience as a loss of relative status, then of course it will be emotionally difficult for you. If, however, you treat a humbling experience as a sign of your having become more aware of the infinite possibilities (both external and internal) that the universe represents, it's not so bad.

This is perhaps one of the greatest applications of "stupidity science." When life hands you one of the those unpleasant "teaching moments," you can fearfully escape into denial and/or curse yourself for "being so dumb," or you can calmly take advantage of the learning opportunity that has appeared. Managing your sense of embarrassment is key to managing any difficult situation. Principle #10 (accepting your inner idiot), and along with it accepting your own human frailty and occasional fallibility, gives you permission to calmly accept the truth. You can see and correct your mistakes and, no matter where you are starting from, ultimately move on to a higher level of existence.

"If you want to improve, be content to be thought foolish and stupid."

–Epictetus

Conclusion

Well here it is, the last chapter of the book. Frankly, I am pretty amazed that I got this far, and I hope you enjoyed this little adventure outside the status quo. And by the way, thank you for buying the book. I really appreciate the business.

Anyway, in lieu of a grand conclusion, here are just a few thoughts that didn't fit into any of the other chapters:

The main purpose of this book was to offer you, dear reader, a clearer and more objective view of just what the words "smart" and "stupid" mean. Hopefully, having greater consciousness and command of the power of these words will give you greater freedom of thought and action.

One item not overtly mentioned was the wondrous benefits of being empty-headed from time to time. Most of us have been taught to accept the most common presumption of smartist dogma, i.e., that thinking and knowledge are good, period. But . . . self-doubt and anxiety are thoughts. A memory of a painful experience is knowledge. Therefore, there are times when mental activity is simply not helpful. The "smartist" solution to every negative thought is always to find yet another thought with which to counter it, but . . . this approach essentially requires you to double your mental workload just to get yourself back to zero. Seems awfully inefficient. So, rather than constantly trying to find yet another thought or piece of information that will counteract a negative thought, it is ever so much easier to simply turn off these negative thoughts and memories in the first place.

The idea that it is okay for you to simply "not think" is completely counter to a lifetime of immersion in smartist dogma. As a result, you may find that it somehow "feels wrong." This gut feeling really is at the heart of the matter; the essence of "stupidity science" is not *how* to do it, as, with just a little bit of logic and/or repeated effort, the *how* is ridiculously easy. Stupidity science is simply the *permission* to do it . . . or perhaps we should we say, permission *not* do it, e.g., not think so much all the time.

One almost grand discovery that grew out of the writing of this book was seeing the bigger picture of where these cultural concepts of "smart" and "stupid" come from. There are repeated analogies between what we have all been taught is "smart" and "stupid" and what is good and what is not good for the greater efficiency of a factory or a bureaucracy. High speed, efficiency, obedience, uniformity, neatness, pleasing authority, seeking perfection, the ability to memorize, the entire group meeting the same minimum standards, everyone giving the same expected predetermined answer . . . these "smart" attributes are very handy if you're working in a factory. Unfortunately, most of the factories have moved to Asia. The old system is no longer applicable in a thought-worker world. It no longer makes sense to embed this highly limiting matrix of arbitrary emotional associations. "Smartness" is obsolete. We would be much better off standing back and allowing more variation, creativity, experimentation, and leadership.

All too often, in the name of chasing an abstract ideal of "smartness," we are really just creating emotional armor and concealing our vulnerable and imperfect inner selves. While many will tell you that this perfectionist intellectual armor we take on is a source of power, in reality, it is a suppression and abandonment of the most powerful and beautiful parts of ourselves.

The high degree of emotion we associate with our being seen as "smart" or "dumb" is not innate–it is indicative of fear, or even emotional trauma. It's time to ask if the stress we create to motivate "smart" behavior is worth what it costs us in terms of chronic stress, anxiety, interpersonal conflict, and the deep sense of personal inadequacy that so many people silently take away from it.

And finally, of all the limiting forms of intelligence, perhaps the worst is being an expert in surviving in an unhealthy environment. As difficult as some personal or professional situations may be, it is often more comfortable to stay in that environment. No matter how awful a given situation might be, it has the advantage of being "the devil you know." When you know the rules of those environments, you can at least feel somewhat "smart" if you remain there. If you were to move to a new and better place, you might encounter the feeling of being less experienced, and therefore you might feel "dumb." So in a sense, the desire to be smart, combined with the desire to avoid feeling dumb, is one of the most limiting factors in life.

Once you break free of the standard narrow templates of smart and stupid, and you create a broader acceptance of your own mental complexity and its constantly shifting focus, and you understand that you can accept or ignore other people's frames of reference without feeling put upon, judged, or threatened, well, guess what? The next big step is, you can start to ignore your own old frames of reference and create new ones. This is one of the greatest powers of Applied Stupidity. It frees you from the bondage of pride in something either useless or limiting (most notably, your expertise in your own past), and gives you the power and freedom to totally change your life if you feel the need to do so.

It might seem strange to think you could do something so positive with a force that is normally thought of as being so negative. "Stupidity is a good and useful thing? Are you nuts?" The first caveman to suggest bringing fire into the cave probably encountered a similar reaction.

And one final note: in case of the unlikely possibility that you may be thinking that I am somehow smarter than you are just because I wrote a book, I hope you will now envision me lying on a couch, in a creme de menthe induced stupor, saying to you,

"Sounds great—play some more."

For your next event: Justin Locke is a unique and entertaining speaker. You can find about more about him (and you can also order copies of this and his other books and publications) by visiting his website at

www.justinlocke.com

*   *   *

There is never any reason to slog through the "acknowledgments" at the front of a book unless you are one of the people being acknowledged, so I didn't put this at the top. However, I did want to say a few thank-you's.

First of all, thanks to Kate Alley and Ralph Loftin for suffering through some truly gruesome early drafts, and making me aware of some really bad things I was doing.

Second, many thanks to Mary Francica for offering much-needed encouragement, and special thanks to my brother Joseph, who also offered much-needed encouragement, and who also contributed heavily both to the book's content and to its "voice."

I would also like to thank Mary Richardson, Clint Conley, and all the folks at WCVB-TV who were kind enough to feature this book on *Chronicle*. And I would also like to say an ongoing "thank you" to all the folks who have reviewed the book, and those who invite me to speak to their companies and organizations about this decidedly unusual topic.

The Principles of Applied Stupidity:

Principle #1:
The *Absence* of Thought and Information
Is Just as Powerful as the
***Presence* of Thought and Information**

Principle #2:
Everyone Is a Genius.

Principle #3:
"Stupid" Does Not Mean Stupid.

Principle #4:
"Smart" Does Not Mean Smart.

Principle #5:
The Fear of Looking Stupid Is an Enormous Force.

Principle #6:
Everyone Wants to Look and Feel Smart.

Principle #7:
Stupidity and Ignorance Are Infinite.

Principle #8:
There Is Nothing Wrong with Being Stupid.

Principle #9:
Knowledge Is Often Counterproductive.

Principle #10:
Embrace Your Inner Idiot

Principle #11:
The Less Thinking a Manager Does,
the More Thinking the People
Who Work for That Manager
Have to Do, and Vice Versa.

Principle #12:
Information Flows from Smart to Dumb.

Principle #13:
Letting People Feel Smarter than You
Makes You Look Even Smarter to Them.

Principle #14:
Imagining That Other People Are "Smarter" than
You Are Makes You a Better Listener,
and Therefore More Effective in All of Your
Interactions and Communications.

Principle #15:
Slowness of Mind, Not Quickness,
Puts You in Charge.

Principle #16:
Imminent Disaster, Whether Real, Contrived,
or Just Perceived, Is a Universal Motivator.

Principle #17:
Procedures Are Not Designed to Find People,
They Are Designed to Get Rid of Them.

Principle #18:
The Minimum Is the Maximum.

Principle # 19:
People Are So Fascinated by Large Mistakes That
They Will Fail to Notice Little Mistakes,
or Anything Else for That Matter
(a.k.a. The Irregardless Effect).

Principle #20:
Stupidity Is a Breeding Ground for
New Ideas and Innovation in General.

Principle #21:
Stupidity Is Better than Anxiety.

Principle #22:
Sometimes, Ignoring a Problem
DOES Make it Go Away All by Itself.

Principle #23:
The Choice Is Not Between Being Smart or
Dumb. The Choice Is Between Being
Effective or Ineffective.

Principle #24:
For Every Goal You Can See,
There Is Another One That You Can't See.

Principle #25:
Tests Only Measure Your Ability to
Take the Test You Are Taking.

Principle #26:
The Correctness of an Answer to a
Question Is Never Absolute and Is
Always Affected by Who Is Giving the Test.

Principle #27:
Cheating Means Breaking the Rules,
and Different Games Have Different Rules.

Principle #28:
Even the Smartest People in the World Have Finite
Amounts of Intelligence and Knowledge. Their
Ignorance Outweighs Their Intelligence by
Miles and Miles.

Principle #29:
"I Don't Know" Is an Acceptable Answer.

Principle #30:
When Smart Meets Dumb, Dumb Always Wins.

Principle #31:
Failures are Derived from Arbitrary Standards.

Principle #32:
Failure Is Good.

Principle #33:
Let Other People Solve the Problem.

Principle #34:
Ignorance of Difficulty = Optimism.

Have Justin Locke speak at your next event or management meeting! For more info visit www.justinlocke.com.

If you enjoyed reading this book, we hope you will tell your friends. Word-of-mouth is our best form of advertising!

You might also enjoy reading Justin Locke's humorous musical memoir, "Real Men Don't Rehearse."

Visit www.justinlocke.com for info on how to order books, view videos, give feedback, read updates, and see schedules of Justin's upcoming speaking appearances.

Thank you very much for your business!